365 Easy Soups & Stews

Simple, Delicious Recipes to Warm the Heart

365 Easy Soups and Stews

1st Printing   October 2006

2nd Printing   February 2007

ISBN: 9781931294263

Library of Congress Number: 2006934670

Illustrations by Nancy Bohanan

Edited, Designed and Published in the
United States of America by
Cookbook Resources, LLC
541 Doubletree Drive
Highland Village, Texas 75077
Toll free 866-229-2665
www.cookbookresources.com

Ladle Up Comfort With Soup

Nothing says home and comfort more than a big pot of homemade soup simmering gently on the stove. Soups and stews are one of life's great comforts. They are warming, brimming with flavor and bring back sweet memories of mom's chicken noodle soup, the one soup that always seemed to make even the worst cold vanish. There's just something about soup that makes everything seem better.

Thick or thin, hot or cold, subtle or spicy, brothy or chunky – **365 Easy Soups and Stews** has a soup to fit any mood and every taste. From cover to cover simple, delicious recipes can help make family meals into "feel-good" meals. These soups, stews, chilis and chowders help build family favorites and family traditions.

Warm your kitchen and your heart with **Zesty Creamy Chicken Soup** on page 27, a surprisingly easy recipe for a fast chicken soup. Or try a big rich bowl of **Incredible Broccoli-Cheese Soup** on page 162. And it doesn't get any easier than **Easy Chunky Chili** on page 90, chock-full of a medley of beefy stew meat, vegetables and spices. Our collection of recipes for soups and stews makes it possible to ladle up a bowl of soup every day of the

CONTENTS

CONTENTS

Simmering Soups for Centuries

Our prehistoric ancestors, who were forced to stalk and kill their dinner before they could even think about cooking it, discovered how to mingle meats and vegetables with water before there was even a pot or kettle to cook them in! They did it for survival – a way to feed the old and toothless members of their tribes.

Elderly Neanderthal skeletons were found in France with teeth worn down below gum level. They could only have been kept alive through the compassion of tribe members who found a food alternative to indigestible plants and tough meats.

Historians believe that man knew how to boil well before 6,000 B.C. when earthenware pottery was discovered. Prehistoric man found that reptile shells and animal hides made perfect vessels to boil liquid filled with fresh meat. Evidence including residue sticking to pots indicates that our ancestors were regularly eating soup by the Iron and Bronze Ages.

The origins of the word "soup" go back to broth. Deriving from Old English, broth served over bread in a bowl was called "sop" or "sup." From this, the word "soup" evolved. In French, it is "soupe;" in Spanish, "sopa," and in Dutch, "soep." In English it's soup and we've **365 Easy Soups and Stews** just for you.

Satisfying Summer Soups

Cold Peach Soup

This is a beautiful and delicious soup to serve as a first course at a ladies' luncheon or gathering of friends.

1 ½ pounds fresh peaches, peeled, sliced	.7 kg
1 (8 ounce) carton sour cream	227 g
1 (8 ounce) carton peach yogurt	227 g
2 ½ cups orange juice	600 ml
1 tablespoon lemon juice	15 ml
3 tablespoons sugar	45 ml

- In blender or food processor, puree peaches until smooth. Add sour cream, yogurt, orange juice and lemon juice and process until they blend well. Stir in sugar, cover and chill at least 2 hours.

Edna Earle's Cold Peach Soup

This is delicious for summer luncheons with vegetables or chicken-salad sandwiches.

2 pounds peaches	1 kg
1 tablespoon lemon juice	15 ml
3 tablespoons quick-cooking tapioca	45 ml
3 tablespoons sugar	45 ml
1 (6 ounce) can frozen orange juice concentrate	168 g

- Puree peaches with lemon juice and set aside. Combine tapioca, sugar, a little salt and 1 cup (240 ml) water. Heat to full boil in saucepan and stir constantly until mixture thickens.

- Transfer to medium bowl. Stir in orange juice until it melts. Add 1½ cups (360 ml) water and stir until smooth. Mix in pureed peaches, cover and chill. Serve cold.

TIP: Make this soup ahead of time so it has time to chill.

Pat's Chilled Strawberry Soup

2 (10 ounce) packages strawberries in syrup	2 (280 g)
½ cup cranberries	120 ml
2 (8 ounce) cartons strawberry yogurt	2 (227 g)

- Combine all ingredients in blender and mix until smooth.
- Chill 1 to 2 hours before serving.

Luncheon Fruit Soup

¾ cup sugar	180 ml
4 tablespoons quick-cooking tapioca	60 ml
¼ teaspoon ground cinnamon	1 ml
1 (6 ounce) can frozen orange juice concentrate, thawed	168 g
2 cups frozen, sliced peaches, thawed	480 ml
1 (15 ounce) can pear slices with juice	425 g
1 (8 ounce) can crushed pineapple with juice	227 g
1 (16 ounce) package sliced, sweetened strawberries, thawed	.5 kg

- Combine sugar, tapioca and cinnamon and 3 cups (710 ml) water in large saucepan. Cook over medium heat and stir constantly for about 10 minutes or until mixture thickens. Remove from heat and pour in orange juice concentrate.

- Cut peaches and pears into bite-size pieces. Stir peaches, pears, pineapple and strawberries into tapioca-orange juice mixture. Cover and chill at least 2 hours.

Cold Strawberry Soup

2 ¼ cups strawberries	540 ml
⅓ cup sugar	80 ml
½ cup sour cream	120 ml
½ cup whipping cream	120 ml
½ cup light red wine	120 ml

- Puree strawberries and sugar in blender. Pour into pitcher, stir in sour cream and whipping cream and blend well.

- Add red wine and 1¼ cups (300 ml) water. Stir and chill before serving.

Chilled Summertime Soup

3 cups chilled, cubed fresh cantaloupe, divided	710 ml
3 cups chilled, cubed fresh honeydew melon	710 ml
2 cups chilled, fresh orange Juice	480 ml
2 cups chilled, white wine or champagne	480 ml
¼ cup chilled, fresh lime juice	60 ml
3 tablespoons honey	45 ml

- Puree 2 cups (480 ml) cantaloupe in food processor or blender and pour into large bowl. Puree honeydew melon and combine with pureed cantaloupe, orange juice, white wine and lime juice.

- Pour in honey and mix well. Chop remaining cantaloupe and add to bowl. Serve immediately. Serves 8.

  TIP: *Fresh mint as garnish is always a nice touch.*

Strawberry-Orange Soup

1 ½ cups fresh strawberries	360 ml
1 cup orange juice	240 ml
¼ cup honey	60 ml
½ cup sour cream	120 ml
½ cup white wine	120 ml

- Combine all ingredients in blender and puree.

- Chill thoroughly. Stir before pouring into individual soup bowls.

Summer Breeze Raspberry Soup

3 ½ cups fresh raspberries	830 ml
1 cup rose wine	240 ml
¾ cup sugar	180 ml
1 cup sour cream	240 ml

- Mash raspberries, mix in blender and strain to remove seeds. Add enough water to make 3 ½ cups (830 ml). Place raspberry mixture, wine, sugar and salt to taste in saucepan.

- Bring to a boil, reduce heat, cover and simmer for 5 minutes. Cool, add sour cream and stir until it blends thoroughly. Chill about 4 hours.

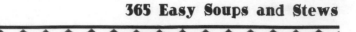

Chilled Yogurt Soups

Here are two light, chilled soups that are unusually good. Yogurt has a unique flavor and gives soups a delicious, tangy taste. Both of these soups are prepared the same way, but one uses cucumber and one uses avocados.

Chilled Yogurt Soup With Cucumbers

4 cucumbers, peeled, seeded, divided
3 cups plain yogurt   710 ml
1 tablespoon minced onion   15 ml

- Place 3 cucumbers, yogurt and onion in food processor or blender and process until just smooth. Salt to taste, cover and chill for several hours.

- Chill soup bowls at the same time and pour soup into bowls when ready to serve. Thinly slice remaining cucumber and garnish soup with several slices.

Chilled Yogurt Soup With Avocados

4 ripe avocados, peeled, seeded, divided
3 cups plain yogurt   710 ml
1 tablespoon minced onion   15 ml

- Place 3 avocados, yogurt and onion in food processor or blender and process until just smooth. Salt to taste, cover and chill for several hours.

- Chill soup bowls at the same time and pour soup into bowls when ready to serve. Thinly slice remaining avocado and garnish soup with several slices.

Vichyssoise

¼ cup (½ stick) butter	60 ml
1 onion, chopped	
3 medium potatoes, peeled, sliced	
2 (14 ounce) cans chicken broth	2 (396 g)
2 cups milk	480 ml
1 (8 ounce) carton whipping cream	227 g

- Melt butter and saute onion in large soup pot. Add sliced potatoes and chicken broth and boil. Reduce heat and simmer about 35 minutes or until potatoes are tender.

- Place about half soup mixture in blender, process until smooth and return to soup pot. Repeat with remaining soup mixture. Stir constantly and add milk, ½ teaspoon (2 ml) pepper and salt to taste. Cover and heat on medium until thoroughly hot. Cool.

- Stir in whipping cream, cover and chill. Serve in chilled individual bowls or cover and refrigerate up to 24 hours.

    TIP: *A parsley garnish is a nice touch, but not a "must".*

Check seasonings of cold soups just before serving because chilled foods tend to dull the taste buds and will need more seasoning than hot soups.

Easy Gazpacho

2 (28 ounce) cans diced tomatoes   2 (794 g)
1 seedless cucumber, peeled, cubed
1 cup chopped red onion   240 ml
1 cup chopped celery   240 ml
2 serrano chile peppers, seeded,
   coarsely chopped

- Work in batches to combine all ingredients plus a little salt and pepper in food processor and pulse until mixture is thick.

- Garnish with several lemon slices, if desired.

   TIP: Use rubber gloves to work with peppers.

White Gazpacho

¼ cup packed parsley leaves   80 ml
3 cloves garlic, chopped
1 teaspoon dried basil   5 ml
1 teaspoon dried oregano   5 ml
3 seedless cucumbers, peeled, chopped
1 green bell pepper, seeded, quartered
1 white onion, quartered
2 (8 ounce) cartons plain yogurt   2 (227 g)
2 (14 ounce) cans chicken broth   2 (396 g)
2 tablespoons lemon juice   30 ml
Hot sauce

- Finely chop parsley and add garlic, basil and oregano. Place cucumbers, green pepper and onion in blender, process until coarsely chopped and add parsley mixture.

- Stir in yogurt, broth, lemon juice and ½ teaspoon (2 ml) each of salt and pepper and mix well. Season to taste with hot sauce and chill.

Rio Grande Gazpacho

This spicy vegetable soup made from a puree of raw vegetables is served cold and is great in the summer.

1 cucumber, peeled, seeded, quartered	
1 bell pepper, seeded, quartered	
½ onion, quartered	
1 teaspoon minced garlic	5 ml
2 teaspoons chopped fresh parsley	10 ml
3 ¼ cups tomato juice, divided	770 ml
1 pound tomatoes, peeled, quartered, cored	.5 kg
¼ cup sliced pimento-stuffed olives	60 ml
3 tablespoons red wine vinegar	45 ml
1 tablespoons olive oil	15 ml
½ teaspoon cumin	2 ml
½ teaspoon oregano	2 ml
2 teaspoons hot sauce	10 ml

- Combine cucumber, bell pepper, onion, garlic, parsley and 2 cups (480 ml) tomato juice in blender. Process until vegetables are coarsely chopped. Add tomatoes and process again until vegetables are finely chopped.

- Pour into medium container with tight lid. Stir in olives, wine vinegar, olive oil, ½ teaspoon (2 ml) salt, cumin, oregano and hot sauce.

- Stir in remaining tomato juice, cover and chill 24 hours. Serve cold.

For cold soups, chill your soup bowls so that the soup remains cold longer.

Chilled Squash Soup

2 pounds yellow squash, thinly sliced	**1 kg**
1 onion, chopped	
1 (14 ounce) can chicken broth	**396 g**
1 (8 ounce) package cream cheese, softened	**227 g**

- Combine squash, onion and broth in saucepan and boil. Cover, reduce heat and simmer for 10 minutes or until tender. Set aside until slightly cool.

- Spoon half squash mixture and half cream cheese into blender. Process until smooth and stop once to scrape down sides. Repeat procedure.

- Stir in salt and pepper to taste and chill.

Gazpacho

2 large ripe tomatoes, chopped, drained	
1 yellow onion, finely chopped	
1 seedless cucumber, peeled, chopped	
1 teaspoon minced garlic	**5 ml**
1 (7 ounce) jar roasted red bell peppers, drained	**198 g**
1 (48 ounce) can tomato juice	**1.3 kg**
¼ cup lime juice	**60 ml**
¼ cup red wine vinegar	**60 ml**
2 tablespoons olive oil	**30 ml**
½ teaspoon sugar	**2 ml**
1 teaspoon hot sauce	**5 ml**

- Process tomatoes, onion, cucumber, garlic and roasted bell peppers in food processor or blender.

- Stir puree, tomato juice, lime juice, vinegar, oil, sugar, hot sauce and salt and pepper to taste. Cover and chill at least 4 hours.

Artichoke Soup

3 tablespoons butter	45 ml
2 tablespoons finely minced green onions	30 ml
1 ½ tablespoons flour	22 ml
2 (14 ounce) cans chicken broth	2 (396 g)
1 (16 ounce) can artichoke bottoms, drained	.5 kg
1 cup half-and-half cream	240 ml

- Melt butter in large saucepan and saute green onions. Stir in flour and cook for 3 minutes. Slowly add broth, stir constantly and cook on medium heat until mixture thickens. Puree artichokes in blender and stir into broth mixture plus salt and pepper to taste. Add cream and heat just until soup is thoroughly hot.

- This soup may be served hot or cold, therefore when serving cold, do not heat after adding cream. Chill 2 hours before serving.

Cucumber Dill Soup

3 medium cucumbers, peeled, seeded, cubed	
1 (14 ounce) can chicken broth, divided	396 g
1 (8 ounce) carton sour cream	227 g
3 tablespoons fresh chives, minced	45 ml
2 teaspoons fresh dill, minced	10 ml

- Combine cucumbers, 1 cup (240 ml) chicken broth and salt to taste in blender. Cover and process until smooth. Transfer to medium bowl and stir in remaining chicken broth.

- Whisk in sour cream, chives and dill. Cover and chill well before serving. Garnish with dill sprig.

Asparagus Chiller

1 (10 ounce) can cream of asparagus soup	280 g
⅔ cup sour cream	160 ml
½ cup finely chopped cucumber	120 ml
2 tablespoons chopped red onion	30 ml

- Blend soup, sour cream and ¾ soup can water in bowl. Stir in cucumber and onion.

- Chill for at least 4 hours and serve in chilled bowls.

Easy Yogurt-Cucumber Chiller

1 pint plain yogurt	.5 kg
1 (10 ounce) can chicken broth	280 g
1 lemon	
¾ cup cucumber, peeled, seeded, grated	180 ml
¼ cup whipping cream	60 ml
1 teaspoon finely chopped green onion with tops	5 ml
½ teaspoon chopped fresh dill	2 ml

- Add yogurt to chicken broth in large bowl and mix well. Cut lemon in half and squeeze 1 teaspoon (5 ml) juice into broth mixture. Cut very thin slices from other half and chill.

- Add remaining ingredients with a little salt and pepper to taste and stir until soup blends well. Chill at least 4 hours. Before serving, place 1 slice lemon on top of each serving.

Chilled Cucumber Soup

2 seedless cucumbers, peeled
½ cup buttermilk, divided*   120 ml
½ cup sour cream   120 ml
2 teaspoons white vinegar   10 ml
1 teaspoon olive oil   5 ml
1 teaspoon sugar   5 ml
½ teaspoon dried dill, crumbled   2 ml

- Coarsely chop cucumbers and place cucumbers and ¼ cup (60 ml) buttermilk in blender or food processor and puree. Transfer to bowl and whisk in remaining ingredients with salt and pepper to taste.

- Cover bowl, refrigerate 30 minutes and stir occasionally. Serve in chilled bowls.

    TIP: To make buttermilk, mix 1 cup (240 ml) milk with 1 tablespoon lemon juice or vinegar and let milk rest about 10 minutes.

Quick Borscht

1 (15 ounce) jar whole red beets   425 g
1 (14 ounce) can beef broth   396 g
4 tablespoons sour cream   60 ml

- Drain beets and save liquid. Chop beets and combine with beet liquid and broth in saucepan. Heat for 10 minutes.

- Chill and serve with dollop of sour cream.

Creamy Cucumber Soup

2 seedless cucumbers, peeled, coarsely chopped	
2 green onions, coarsely chopped	
1 tablespoon lemon juice	15 ml
1 pint half-and-half cream	.5 kg
1 (8 ounce) carton sour cream	227 g
1 teaspoon dried dillweed	5 ml

- Process cucumbers, onions and lemon juice in blender until mixture is smooth. Transfer pureed mixture to bowl with lid.

- Gently stir in cream, sour cream, dillweed, 1 teaspoon (5 ml) salt and ½ teaspoon (2 ml) pepper. Add a dash of hot sauce, if you like.

- Cover and refrigerate several hours before serving. Stir mixture well before serving in soup bowls.

Sweet Carrot Soup

1 (16 ounce) package shredded carrots	.5 kg
1 cup orange juice	240 ml
1 cup apricot nectar	240 ml
¼ cup lemon juice	60 ml
⅓ cup honey	80 ml
⅓ cup sour cream	80 ml

- Combine carrots, orange juice, apricot nectar and ½ cup (120 ml) water in large saucepan. Boil, reduce heat and simmer 20 minutes.

- Add lemon juice, honey and sour cream and stir well. Serve soup at room temperature or chilled.

Fresh Avocado Soup

3 ripe avocados
4 tablespoons fresh lemon juice 60 ml
1 (10 ounce) can chicken broth 280 g
1 (8 ounce) carton plain yogurt 227 g
Chopped chives

- Peel avocados, remove seeds and cut into pieces.
  Immediately put avocados, lemon juice, broth and yogurt
  into blender and process until smooth.

- Add salt and pepper to taste
  and chill several hours. Serve
  in soup bowls with chopped
  chives on top.

Avocado-Cream Soup

4 large, ripe avocados, peeled, diced, divided
1 ½ cups whipping cream, divided 360 ml
2 (14 ounce) cans chicken broth 2 (396 g)
¼ cup dry sherry 60 ml

- Puree 2 avocados and half whipping cream in blender.
  Repeat with remaining avocados and cream.

- Bring chicken broth to boil, reduce heat and stir in avocado
  puree. Add 1 teaspoon (5 ml) salt and sherry and chill
  thoroughly. Serve in chilled soup bowls.

Who's Who: Soups, Stews, Chowders and Chilis

Soups and Stews
Most of us know or have a pretty good idea of the difference between **soups** and **stews**. **Soups are thin and stews are thick**. It's very simple. But, if you want to know more about these comforting dishes, look deeper to find out many other differences.

Soups start with liquid usually hot water. Meats, beans and vegetables are boiled to extract the flavors of the ingredients and that is the broth or stock used as the base. As the boil they break down and mix with the liquid for a distinctive blend of flavors.

Clear soups are called broth, bouillon or consommé. Purees are mixes of vegetables and liquid thickened by the starch in the vegetables. Other types of purees are thickened with cream, milk, eggs, rice, flour or grains.

Stews are very similar to **soups** because they are combinations of vegetables and meats cooked in a broth or stock. They are thickened with most of the same ingredients as **soups**, but there is a distinct difference. **Stews** usually have larger pieces of meat and vegetables than do **soups**. These large pieces are boiled, covered and simmered for a long time to tenderize the ingredients.

Stews are usually served as a main course and **soups** are usually served as a first course. **Stews** are usually heartier and more filling than **soups**, but there is little difference in the popularity of both.

Chowders are similar to stews, but mainly consist of fish or clams, potatoes and onions. New England clam **chowder** has a cream base and Manhattan clam **chowder** has a tomato base. There is also corn **chowder** with a cream base.

Chile with an "e" refers to the many peppers available for cooking. **Chili** with an "i" refers to the state dish of Texas where it originated. Dallas' Frank Tolbert, the founder of the International Terlingua Chili Cook-off and chili aficionado, called **chili** "a bowl of red" to reflect the proper color of the dish.

Chicken Chill-Chasers

County's Best Chicken Soup

4 boneless, skinless chicken breast halves	
3 (14 ounce) cans chicken broth	3 (396 g)
2 tablespoons butter	30 ml
3 medium red potatoes, cut into wedges	
2 ribs celery, chopped	
1 carrot, peeled, shredded	
1 (10 ounce) package frozen green peas	280 g
1 (10 ounce) package frozen corn	280 g
1 ½ cups buttermilk*	360 ml
½ cup flour	120 ml
½ teaspoon cayenne pepper	2 ml
1 teaspoon Worcestershire sauce	5 ml

- Bring chicken and broth to boil in large saucepan and cook for 10 minutes or until done. Remove chicken with slotted spoon and save broth. Cut chicken into bite-size pieces.

- Melt butter in soup pot, add potatoes and saute about 5 minutes. Add reserved broth, chicken, celery, shredded carrot, peas and corn and simmer for 30 minutes.

- Stir together buttermilk and flour until smooth, add to chicken-potato mixture and cook, stirring constantly, for 5 minutes. Stir in cayenne pepper and Worcestershire sauce.

TIP: To make buttermilk, mix 1 cup (240 ml) milk with 1 tablespoon lemon juice or vinegar and let milk rest about 10 minutes.

All-American Soup

3 boneless, skinless chicken breast halves, cut into strips	
1 onion, chopped	
1 (10 ounce) can tomatoes and green chilies	280 g
2 (14 ounce) cans chicken broth	2 (396 g)
3 large baking potatoes, peeled, cubed	
1 (10 ounce) can cream of celery soup	280 g
1 cup milk	240 ml
1 teaspoon dried basil	5 ml
1 (8 ounce) package shredded processed cheese	227 g
½ cup sour cream	120 ml

- Brown and cook chicken strips and onion in large saucepan with a little oil about 10 minutes. Add tomatoes and green chilies, chicken broth and cubed potatoes. Boil and cook for 15 minutes or until potatoes are tender.

- Stir in soup, milk, basil, 1 teaspoon (5 ml) salt and pepper to taste. Cook on medium heat and stir constantly until thoroughly hot.

- Stir in cheese until cheese melts. Remove from heat and stir in sour cream.

Americans consume more than 10 billion bowls of soup every year.

Creamy Broccoli-Rice Soup

1 (6 ounce) package chicken and wild rice mix	168 g
1 (10 ounce) package chopped broccoli	280 g
2 (10 ounce) cans cream of chicken soup	2 (280 g)
1 (12 ounce) can chicken breast chunks	340 g

- Combine rice mix, contents of seasoning packet and 5 cups (1.3 L) water in soup pot. Boil, reduce heat and simmer for 15 minutes.

- Stir in broccoli, chicken soup and chicken. Cover and simmer for another 5 minutes.

Chicken-Veggie Soup

1 (32 ounce) carton chicken broth	1 kg
2 small carrots, thinly sliced	
1 rib celery, diced	
1 baby leek, halved lengthwise, sliced	
1 (8 ounce) can peas	227 g
1 cup cooked rice	240 ml
1 cup cooked, sliced chicken	240 ml
2 teaspoons chopped fresh tarragon	10 ml

- Pour stock in large saucepan and add carrots, celery and leek. Boil, reduce heat and simmer, partially covered, for 10 minutes.

- Stir in peas, rice and chicken and continue cooking for 10 to 15 minutes or until vegetables are tender. Add chopped tarragon and salt and pepper to taste.

Zesty Creamy Chicken Soup

This is a really easy way to whip up a fast chicken soup.

2 tablespoons (¼ stick) butter	30 ml
½ onion, finely chopped	
1 carrot, grated	
1 (10 ounce) can cream of celery soup	280 g
1 (10 ounce) can cream of mushroom soup	280 g
1 (10 ounce) can cream of chicken soup	280 g
1 (14 ounce) can chicken broth	396 g
2 soup cans milk	
1 tablespoon parsley flakes	15 ml
¼ teaspoon garlic powder	1 ml
1 (16 ounce) package mild, cubed Mexican processed cheese	.5 kg
4 boneless, skinless chicken breast halves, cooked, diced	

- Melt butter and saute onion and carrots in large saucepan or roasting pan for 10 minutes, but do not brown. Add remaining ingredients and heat but do not boil.

- Reduce heat to low, cook until cheese melts and stir constantly. Serve piping hot.

TIP: This is really the "easy" way to make chicken soup and if you are in an absolute rush, you could even use 2 (12 ounces/340g) cans chicken. Leftover turkey could be substituted for chicken.

Cheesy Chicken Soup

1 (10 ounce) can fiesta nacho cheese soup	280 g
1 (10 ounce) can cream of chicken soup	280 g
1 soup can milk	280 g
1 (12 ounce) can chicken breasts with liquid	340 g

• Mix all ingredients in saucepan on medium heat and stir until thoroughly hot. Serve hot.

Chicken and Rice Gumbo

3 (14 ounce) cans chicken broth	3 (396 g)
1 pound boneless, skinless chicken breasts, cubed	.5 kg
2 (15 ounce) cans whole kernel corn, drained	2 (425 g)
2 (15 ounce) cans stewed tomatoes with liquid	2 9425 g)
¾ cup white rice	180 ml
1 teaspoon Cajun seasoning	5 ml
2 (10 ounce) packages frozen okra, thawed, chopped	2 (280 g)

• On high heat, combine chicken broth and chicken in soup pot and cook for 15 minutes.

• Add remaining ingredients and 1 teaspoon (5 ml) pepper and boil. Reduce heat and simmer for 30 minutes or until rice is done.

Chicken-Rice Soup With Green Chilies

8 boneless, skinless chicken breast halves,
  cooked
2 (14 ounce) cans chicken broth   2 (396 g)
1 cup chopped celery   240 ml
1 cup rice   240 ml
2 - 4 large fresh, green chilies, seeded, chopped

- Cut cooked chicken into small pieces and place in large saucepan.

- Add chicken broth, celery, rice, green chilies, 1 teaspoon (5 ml) salt and ¼ teaspoon (1 ml) pepper and simmer for about 35 minutes or until rice is tender.

Creamy Chicken-Spinach Soup

1 (9 ounce) package refrigerated
  cheese tortellini   255 g
2 (14 ounce) cans chicken broth, divided   2 (396 g)
1 (10 ounce) can cream of chicken soup   280 g
1 (12 ounce) can white chicken meat
  with liquid   340 g
1 (10 ounce) package frozen chopped spinach   280 g
2 cups milk   480 ml
½ teaspoon dried thyme   2 ml

- Cook tortellini in soup pot with 1 can chicken broth according to package directions.

- Stir in remaining can broth, soup, chicken, chopped spinach, milk, 1 teaspoon (5 ml) salt, ½ teaspoon (2 ml) pepper and thyme. Boil, reduce heat to low and simmer for 10 minutes.

Cold Night Bean Soup

1 ½ cups dried navy beans	360 ml
3 (14 ounce) cans chicken broth	3 (396 g)
4 tablespoons (½ stick) butter	60 ml
1 onion, chopped	
1 clove garlic, minced	
3 cups chopped, cooked chicken	710 ml
1 (4 ounce) can chopped green chilies	114 g
1 ½ teaspoons ground cumin	7 ml
½ teaspoon cayenne pepper	2 ml
Grated Monterey Jack cheese	

- Sort, wash beans and place in soup pot. Cover with water 2 inches (5 cm) above beans and soak overnight.

- Drain beans and add broth, butter, 1 cup (240 ml) water, onion and garlic. Boil, reduce heat and cover. Simmer 2 hours and stir occasionally. Add water if needed.

- With potato masher, mash half the beans. Add chicken, green chilies, cumin and cayenne pepper. Boil, reduce heat and cover. Simmer another 30 minutes.

- When ready to serve, spoon in bowls and top with 1 to 2 tablespoons (15 ml) cheese.

Quick Chicken-Noodle Soup

2 (14 ounce) cans chicken broth	2 (396 g)
2 boneless, skinless chicken breast halves, cubed	
1 (8 ounce) can sliced carrots, drained	227 g
2 ribs celery, sliced	
½ (8 ounce) package uncooked medium egg noodles	227 g

- Combine broth, chicken, carrots, celery and generous dash of pepper in large saucepan. Boil and cook for 3 minutes.

- Stir in noodles, reduce heat and cook for 10 minutes or until noodles are done; stir often.

Feel-Better Chicken-Noodle Soup

1 (3 ounce) package chicken-flavored ramen noodles, broken	84 g
1 (10 ounce) package frozen green peas, thawed	280 g
2 teaspoons butter	10 ml
1 (4 ounce) jar sliced mushrooms, drained	114 g
3 cups cooked, cubed chicken	710 ml

- Heat 2 ¼ cups (540 ml) water in large saucepan to boiling.

- Add ramen noodles, contents of seasoning packet, peas and butter. Heat to boiling, reduce heat to medium and cook about 5 minutes.

- Stir in mushrooms and chicken and continue cooking over low heat until all ingredients heat through. To serve, spoon into serving bowls.

Oriental Chicken-Noodle Soup

1 (3 ounce) package chicken-flavor
  ramen noodles   84 g
1 rotisserie chicken, boned, skinned, cubed
2 medium stalks bok choy with leaves,
  thinly sliced
1 (8 ounce) can sliced carrots, drained   227 g
1 red bell pepper, seeded, chopped

- Break apart noodles, place in 3 cups (710 ml) water and heat in soup pot. Stir in chicken, bok choy, carrots and bell pepper.

- Boil, reduce heat and simmer uncovered for 3 minutes; stir occasionally. Stir in flavor packet from noodles and serve immediately.

Chicken-Veggie Surprise

3 (14 ounce) cans chicken broth   3 (396 g)
1 (15 ounce) can sliced carrots, drained   425 g
1 (15 ounce) can green peas, drained   425 g
1 sweet red bell pepper, seeded, chopped
1 teaspoon dried tarragon   5 ml
½ pound boneless, skinless chicken breasts,
  cooked, cut into strips   227 g
1 (16 ounce) package frozen broccoli florets   .5 kg
4 ounces (about 1 cup) thin egg noodles   114 g/240 ml

- Combine broth, carrots, peas, bell pepper, tarragon and 1 teaspoon (5 ml) salt in large soup pot. Boil, reduce heat and simmer for 5 minutes.

- Add chicken strips and broccoli and cook another 10 minutes. Stir in noodles, boil, reduce heat to medium and cook for 10 minutes or until noodles are tender.

Speedy Gonzales Soup

1 (12 ounce) can chicken with liquid	340 g
1 (14 ounce) can chicken broth	396 g
1 (16 ounce) jar mild thick and chunky salsa	.5 kg
1 (15 ounce) can ranch-style beans	425 g

- Combine chicken, broth, salsa and beans in large saucepan.

- Boil, reduce heat and simmer for 15 minutes.

   TIP: If you have 1 (15 ounce/425 g) can whole kernel corn, add it for a crunchy texture.

Fast Fiesta Soup

1 (15 ounce) can Mexican-style stewed tomatoes	425 g
1 (15 ounce) can whole kernel corn	425 g
1 (15 ounce) can pinto beans with liquid	425 g
2 (14 ounce) cans chicken broth	2 (396 g)
1 (10 ounce) can fiesta nacho soup	280 g
1 (12 ounce) can chicken breast with liquid	340 g

- Combine tomatoes, corn, beans, broth and nacho soup in large soup pot, heat 10 minutes over medium heat and mix well.

- Stir in chicken with liquid and heat until thoroughly hot.

Tempting Tortilla Soup

Don't let the number of ingredients keep you from serving this. It's really easy.

3 large boneless, skinless chicken breast halves, cooked, cubed	
1 (10 ounce) package frozen corn, thawed	280 g
1 onion, chopped	
3 (14 ounce) cans chicken broth	3 (396 g)
2 (10 ounce) cans tomatoes and green chilies	2 (280 g)
2 teaspoons ground cumin	10 ml
1 teaspoon chili powder	5 ml
1 clove garlic, minced	
6 corn tortillas	

- Combine all ingredients except tortillas in large soup pot. Boil, reduce heat and simmer for 35 minutes.

- Preheat oven to 350° (176° C).

- While soup simmers, cut tortillas into 1-inch (2.5 cm) strips and place on baking sheet. Bake about 5 minutes or until crisp. Serve tortilla strips with each serving of soup.

La Placita Enchilada Soup

6 boneless, skinless chicken breast halves	
½ cup (1 stick) butter	120 ml
2 cloves garlic, minced	
1 onion, minced	
⅓ cup flour	180 ml
1 (15 ounce) can Mexican stewed tomatoes, chopped	425 g
1 (7 ounce) can chopped green chilies	198 g
1 (1 pint) carton sour cream	.5 kg
1 (8 ounce) package shredded cheddar cheese	227 g

- Cook chicken with 12 cups (3 L) water in large saucepan until tender. Reserve broth, cube chicken and set aside. In large roasting pan, melt butter and cook garlic and onion until tender.

- Add 1 teaspoon (5 ml) salt to flour, slowly pour flour into butter mixture and stir constantly to dissolve all lumps.

- Continue stirring and slowly pour in reserved chicken broth. Cook until soup thickens to right consistency.

- Add chicken, tomatoes, green chilies and sour cream. Mix well and heat. Serve in individual bowls and sprinkle with cheese.

Screamin' of Jalapeno Soup

3 carrots, peeled, diced	
2 ribs celery, chopped	
1 green bell pepper, seeded, chopped	
6 tablespoons (¾ stick) butter, divided	90 ml
2 (14 ounce) cans chicken broth	2 (396 g)
3 cups shredded, cooked chicken	710 ml
3 - 5 jalapenos, seeded, chopped	
¼ cup flour	60 ml
1 ½ teaspoons ground cumin	7 ml
1 pint whipping cream	.5 kg

- Combine carrots, celery and bell pepper in large skillet and saute in 4 tablespoons (60 ml) butter.

- Transfer to large soup pot and add chicken broth, shredded chicken and jalapenos (3 for medium heat and 5 for serious heat). Boil, reduce heat and simmer for about 30 minutes.

- In same skillet, melt remaining 2 tablespoons (30 ml) butter and add flour and cumin. Heat mixture on low to medium heat, stirring constantly, make a light brown roux.

- Stir in whipping cream, stirring constantly, but do not boil.

- Pour cream mixture into vegetable-chicken mixture and heat on medium, stirring constantly, just until mixture thickens.

TIP: If you like it extra hot, leave the seeds and veins in the jalapenos. Be sure to wear rubber gloves when you handle with jalapenos.

Sopa De Lima

This is a traditional lime and tortilla soup.

4 - 6 boneless, skinless chicken breast halves
1 onion, minced
1 red bell pepper, seeded, chopped
2 cloves garlic, minced
2 tablespoons canola oil   30 ml
6 limes, divided
3 fresh jalapeno or serrano chilies, seeded,
    minced
3 tomatoes, peeled, seeded, chopped
1 (32 ounce) carton chicken broth   1 kg
8 corn tortillas

- Cook chicken, chop into small pieces and set aside. Cook onion, bell pepper and garlic in saucepan with hot oil until onion is translucent.

- Cut 1 lime in half, juice lime and place 2 rind shells into saucepan. Slice remaining limes and set aside.

- Add chilies, tomatoes and broth, simmer for about 10 minutes and discard lime shells. Season chicken with salt and pepper and add to saucepan.

- Cut tortillas in half and slice into narrow strips. Heat oil in large skillet and cook tortilla strips until crispy. Drain on paper towel and put in warm oven until all strips cook.

- Taste soup for seasonings. Pour into individual soup bowls and put lime slice and tortilla strips on top.

TIP: Be sure to wear rubber gloves when you work with chilies.

Seaside Soup Cancun

4 (14 ounce) cans chicken broth	4 (396 g)
1 bunch fresh cilantro, coarsely chopped	
3 boneless, skinless chicken breast halves	
1 ear fresh corn, cut into 6 rounds	
1 tablespoon ground cumin	15 ml
2 tablespoons butter	30 ml
2 onions, chopped	
1 red bell pepper, thinly sliced	
1 clove garlic, minced	
2 tomatoes, chopped	
1 poblano chile, seeded, chopped	
½ teaspoon sugar	2 ml
4 corn tortillas	
Oil	
4 tablespoons lime juice	60 ml
Sour cream	

- Bring chicken broth to boil in large saucepan over high heat. Add cilantro, chicken, corn and cumin. Cook until chicken and corn are done, about 15 minutes.

- Melt butter in skillet and add onion, bell pepper, garlic and tomatoes. Cook, stirring frequently, for about 10 minutes.

- Cut chile into ¼-inch (.6 cm) rounds and add to skillet. Add tomato mixture and sugar to chicken mixture. Cook another 10 minutes.

- Cut tortillas into thin strips, fry in skillet with oil until crispy and drain. Stir in lime juice and pour soup into serving bowls. Garnish with strips of fried tortillas and 1 heaping tablespoon (15 ml) sour cream.

Zesty Chicken Stew

8 boneless, skinless chicken thighs	
¼ cup flour	60 ml
3 tablespoons olive oil	45 ml
¾ teaspoon dried oregano	4 ml
¾ teaspoon dried basil	4 ml
1 large onion, chopped	
1 cup white cooking wine	240 ml
1 (14 ounce) can chicken broth	396 g
3 medium red potatoes, peeled, diced	
1 (15 ounce) can diced tomatoes, drained	425 g
1 (8 ounce) can sliced carrots, drained	227 g
3 tablespoons chopped fresh cilantro	45 ml
Hot cooked brown rice	

- Lightly dredge chicken in flour and shake to remove excess. Brown chicken in hot oil in large heavy pan over medium to high heat for 4 minutes on each side and set aside.

- Combine oregano, basil and salt and pepper to taste and sprinkle mixture evenly over chicken.

- Saute onion in remaining oil in large pan, stir in wine and cook for 2 minutes. Return chicken to pan and add broth, potatoes, tomatoes and carrots.

- Reduce heat and simmer, stirring occasionally, for 45 minutes. Stir in cilantro and serve over hot cooked rice.

Chicken-Sausage Stew

1 (16 ounce) package frozen stew vegetables	.5 kg
2 (12 ounce) cans chicken breast with liquid	2 (340 g)
½ pound Italian sausage, sliced	227 g
2 (15 ounce) cans Italian stewed tomatoes	2 (425 g)
1 (14 ounce) can chicken broth	396 g
¼ teaspoon cayenne pepper	1 ml
1 cup instant rice, cooked	240 ml

- Combine all ingredients except rice and add salt to taste in large heavy soup pot. Boil, reduce heat and simmer for 25 minutes. Stir in cooked rice during last 5 minutes of cooking time.

Wake-Up Chicken-Rice Stew

2 (12 ounce) cans white chicken meat with liquid	2 (340 g)
2 (14 ounce) cans chicken broth	2 (396 g)
1 (15 ounce) can stewed tomatoes	425 g
½ cup hot salsa	120 ml
2 cups instant brown rice	480 ml
1 (15 ounce) can whole kernel corn	425 g
1 (15 ounce) can cut green beans	425 g
½ teaspoon ground cumin	2 ml
½ teaspoon chili powder	2 ml

- Combine chicken, broth, stewed tomatoes, salsa and rice in heavy soup pot. Boil, reduce heat and simmer for 10 minutes.

- Stir in corn, green beans, cumin, chili powder and salt and pepper to taste. Boil, reduce heat and cook for 5 minutes.

Favorite Chicken-Tomato Stew

1 pound boneless, skinless chicken breast halves, cut into strips	.5 kg
1 onion, chopped	
1 green bell pepper, seeded, chopped	
2 (14 ounce) cans chicken broth	2 (396 g)
2 (15 ounce) cans Mexican stewed tomatoes	2 (425 g)
2 (15 ounce) cans navy beans with liquid	2 (425 g)
1 cup salsa	240 ml
2 teaspoons ground cumin	10 ml
1 ½ cups crushed tortilla chips	360 ml

- Brown and cook chicken in stew pot on medium heat for 10 minutes.

- Add onion, bell pepper, broth, tomatoes, navy beans, salsa, cumin and salt and pepper to taste. Boil, reduce heat and simmer for 25 minutes, stirring often.

- Ladle into individual soup bowls and sprinkle crushed tortilla chips on top of stew. Serve immediately.

Sister's Brunswick Stew

This signature southern dish takes longer than most dishes, but it is so worth it. Cook meat one day and put stew together the next day. You'll have enough to freeze and serve for several meals. It makes an excellent one-dish meal.

1 (2 pound) boneless pork loin	1 kg
3 pounds boneless, skinless chicken pieces	1.3 kg
4 medium potatoes, quartered	
3 (28 ounce) cans stewed, diced tomatoes	3 (794 g)
2 teaspoons sugar	10 ml
1 medium onion, chopped	
2 (16 ounce) packages frozen butterbeans, thawed	2 (.5 kg)
2 (16 ounce) packages frozen sweet corn, thawed	2 (.5 kg)

- Cut pork and chicken into bite-size pieces. Cover with water and cook in stew pot for 1 hour, very slowly or until tender. Skim off excess fat.

- Return meat to broth, add potatoes and cook on medium. When done, mash potatoes to thicken broth. Add tomatoes, sugar, salt and pepper to taste and cook until soupy.

- Add onion and butterbeans. Cook for 10 minutes on low and stir frequently.

- Add corn and cook for 5 minutes. Keep scraping bottom of pan to prevent sticking.

Chicken-Broccoli Chowder

2 (14 ounce) cans chicken broth	2 (396 g)
1 bunch fresh green onions, finely chopped, divided	
1 (10 ounce) package frozen chopped broccoli	280 g
1 ½ cups dry mashed potato flakes	360 ml
2 ½ cups cooked, cut-up chicken breasts	600 ml
1 (8 ounce) package shredded mozzarella cheese	227 g
1 (8 ounce) carton whipping cream	227 g
1 cup milk	240 ml

- Combine broth, half green onions and broccoli in large saucepan. Boil, reduce heat, cover and simmer for 5 minutes.

- Stir in dry potato flakes and mix until they blend well. Add chicken, cheese, cream, milk, 1 cup (240 ml) water and salt and pepper to taste. Heat over medium heat and stir occasionally until hot and cheese melts, about 5 minutes.

- Ladle into individual soup bowls and garnish with remaining chopped green onions.

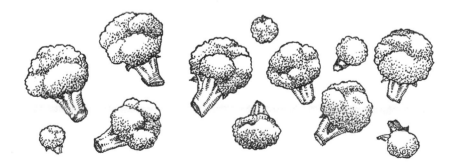

Rich Cheddar Chowder

2 (14 ounce) cans chicken broth	2 (396 g)
4 baking potatoes, peeled, diced	
1 onion, chopped	
1 cup shredded carrots	240 ml
1 green and 1 red bell pepper, seeded, chopped	
¼ cup (½ stick) butter	60 ml
⅓ cup flour	80 ml
1 pint half-and-half cream	.5 kg
1 ½ cups milk	360 ml
1 (16 ounce) package shredded sharp	
cheddar cheese	.5 kg
⅛ - ¼ teaspoon hot sauce	.5 ml

- Combine broth, potatoes, onion, carrots and bell peppers in large soup pot. Bring to boil, reduce heat and simmer for 15 minutes.

- Melt butter in large saucepan, add flour and stir until smooth. Cook 1 minute and stir constantly. Gradually add cream and milk, cook over medium heat and stir constantly until mixture thickens.

- Add cheese and hot sauce to vegetable mixture and cook just until thoroughly hot; do not boil.

Whipped Chicken Chowder

3 cups cooked, cubed chicken	710 ml
1 (14 ounce) can chicken broth	396 g
2 (10 ounce) cans cream of potato soup	2 (280 g)
1 large onion, chopped	
3 ribs celery, sliced diagonally	
1 (16 ounce) package frozen corn, thawed	.5 kg
⅔ cup whipping cream	160 ml

- Combine all ingredients except cream in large soup pot with ¾ cup (180 ml) water.

- Cover and cook on low heat for about 45 minutes. Add whipping cream and heat another 10 minutes on low. Do not boil.

 *The word chowder comes from the French word "chaudiere," a caldron in which fishermen made their stews fresh from the sea. Chowder is a thick, chunky seafood or other thick, rich soup containing chunky food (such as corn chowder). Chowder can contain any of several varieties of seafood and vegetables. New England-style chowder is made with milk or cream and Manhattan-style chowder is made with tomatoes.*

Mama Mia Chicken Chowder

2 (12 ounce) cans chicken breasts with liquid	2 (340 g)
¼ cup Italian salad dressing	60 ml
1 (15 ounce) can stewed tomatoes	425 g
1 (10 ounce) can chicken broth	280 g
2 small zucchini, chopped	
½ cup elbow macaroni	120 ml
1 teaspoon dried basil	5 ml
1 cup shredded mozzarella cheese	240 ml

- Combine chicken, salad dressing, tomatoes, broth, zucchini, macaroni, basil, ½ cup (120 ml) water and salt and pepper to taste in large soup pot.

- Boil, reduce heat and simmer for 10 minutes or until macaroni is tender. Serve in individual soup bowls and sprinkle cheese over each serving.

Cheesy Tomato Chili

1 (28 ounce) can diced tomatoes	794 g
1 (15 ounce) can kidney beans, rinsed, drained	425 g
1 (15 ounce) can pinto beans, drained	425 g
2 (14 ounce) cans chicken broth	2 (396 g)
2 (12 ounce) cans chicken breasts with liquid	2 (340 g)
1 tablespoon chili powder	15 ml
1 (8 ounce) Mexican-style 4-cheese blend, divided	227 g

- Combine tomatoes, kidney beans, pinto beans, broth, chicken, chili powder and salt and pepper to taste. Boil, reduce heat and simmer for 25 minutes.

- Stir in half cheese and spoon into individual soup bowls. Sprinkle remaining cheese on top of each serving.

Great Northern Chili

2 onions, coarsely chopped	
3 (15 ounce) cans great Northern beans, drained	3 (425 g)
2 (14 ounce) cans chicken broth	2 (396 g)
2 tablespoons minced garlic	30 ml
1 (7 ounce) can chopped green chilies	198 g
1 tablespoon ground cumin	15 ml
3 cups cooked, finely chopped chicken breasts	710 ml
1 (8 ounce) package shredded Monterey Jack cheese	227 g

- In large, heavy pot, cook onions in a little oil for about 5 minutes, but do not brown. Place 1 can beans in shallow bowl and mash with fork.

- Add mashed beans, 2 remaining cans of beans, chicken broth, garlic, green chilies and cumin to soup pot. Boil, reduce heat, cover and simmer for 30 minutes.

- Add chopped chicken or deli turkey, stir to blend well and heat until chili is thoroughly hot. When serving, top each bowl with 3 tablespoons (45 ml) cheese.

White Lightning Chili

1 ½ cups dried navy beans	360 ml
3 (14 ounce) cans chicken broth	3 (396 g)
2 tablespoons (¼ stick) butter	30 ml
1 onion, chopped	
1 clove garlic, minced	
3 cups cooked, chopped chicken	710 ml
1 ½ teaspoons ground cumin	7 ml
½ teaspoon cayenne pepper	2 ml
6 (8-inch) flour tortillas	6 (20 cm)
Grated Monterey Jack cheese	

- Sort and wash beans, cover with water and soak overnight. Drain beans and place in soup pot and add broth, butter, 1 cup (240 ml) water, onion and garlic. Boil, reduce heat and cover. Simmer for 2 hours and stir occasionally.

- With potato masher, mash half of beans in soup pot. Add chicken, cumin and cayenne pepper. Boil, reduce heat and cover. Simmer another 30 minutes.

- With kitchen shears, make 4 cuts in each tortilla toward center, but not completely through center. Line serving bowls with tortillas and overlap cut edges. Spoon in chili and top with cheese.

Guess-What Chili

1 (16 ounce) package frozen, chopped onions and bell peppers	.5 kg
2 tablespoons minced garlic	30 ml
2 tablespoons chili powder	30 ml
3 teaspoons ground cumin	15 ml
2 pounds boneless, skinless chicken breast halves, cubed	1 kg
2 (14 ounce) cans chicken broth	2 (396 g)
3 (15 ounce) cans pinto beans with jalapenos, divided	3 (425 g)

- Cook onions and bell peppers in large, heavy soup pot over medium heat with a little oil for about 5 minutes and stir occasionally.

- Add garlic, chili powder, cumin and cubed chicken and cook another 10 minutes. Stir in broth and a little salt. Boil, reduce heat, cover and simmer for 15 minutes.

- Place 1 can beans in shallow bowl and mash with fork. Add mashed beans and remaining 2 cans beans to pot. Boil, reduce heat and simmer for 10 minutes.

TIP: This is delicious served with hot, buttered flour tortillas or spooned over small, original corn chips for a great 1-dish meal.

Make-Believe Chili Supper

1 pound boneless, skinless chicken breast halves, cubed	.5 kg
¼ cup (½ stick) butter	60 ml
3 ribs celery, sliced	
2 onions, chopped	
1 sweet red bell pepper, seeded, chopped	
2 teaspoons minced garlic	10 ml
3 (15 ounce) cans great northern beans with liquid	3 (425 g)
2 (14 ounce) cans chicken broth	2 (396 g)
2 teaspoons ground cumin	10 ml
1 teaspoon dried oregano	5 ml
1 (7 ounce) can chopped green chilies	198 g
1 (8 ounce) carton sour cream	227 g

- Preheat oven to 350° (176° C). Sprinkle 1 teaspoon (5 ml) salt on chicken and place in greased 9 x 13-inch (23 x 33 cm) baking dish and bake for 15 minutes.

- Melt butter and cook celery, onions, bell pepper and garlic in soup pot on medium heat for 10 to 15 minutes.

- Stir in cooked chicken, beans, broth, seasonings and green chilies and mix well. Boil, reduce heat and simmer for 15 minutes. Stir in sour cream.

White Bean Chili

1 pound dried great northern beans	.5 kg
2 onions, finely chopped	
2 ribs celery, sliced	
2 tablespoons olive oil	30 ml
1 (7 ounce) can chopped green chilies	198 g
2 tablespoons minced garlic	30 ml
1 tablespoon ground cumin	15 ml
2 teaspoons dried oregano	10 ml
½ teaspoon cayenne pepper	2 ml
3 (14 ounce) cans chicken broth	3 (396 g)
1 rotisserie chicken, boned, cubed	
1 (12 ounce) package shredded Monterey Jack cheese, divided	340 g

- Sort and rinse beans and place in soup pot. Cover with water 2 inches (5 cm) above beans and soak overnight. Drain beans and set aside.

- In saucepan, saute onions and celery in hot oil. Add green chilies, garlic, cumin, oregano and cayenne pepper, cook 2 minutes and stir constantly.

- Transfer to soup pot and add beans, chicken broth and ½ cup (120 ml) water. Boil and reduce heat. Cover, simmer about 2 hours or until beans are tender; stir occasionally.

- Add chicken and 1 cup (240 ml) cheese. Boil, reduce heat and simmer for 10 minutes, stirring often. Ladle chili into individual soup bowls and top each serving with remaining cheese.

Corny Turkey Soup

¼ cup (½ stick) butter	60 ml
1 small onion, chopped	
1 sweet red bell pepper, seeded, chopped	
1 (3 ounce) package cream cheese, cubed	84 g
1 (15 ounce) can cream-style corn	425 g
1 (15 ounce) can whole kernel corn	425 g
1 (14 ounce) can chicken broth	396 g
½ cup milk	120 ml
2 cups cooked, cubed turkey	480 ml
4 fresh green onions, sliced	

- Melt butter, cook onion and bell pepper in large, heavy soup pot and stir often. On medium heat, add cream cheese and cream-style corn and stir constantly until cheese melts.

- Add whole kernel corn, broth, milk and turkey, mix well and cook until soup is thoroughly hot. Sprinkle sliced green onions over top of each serving.

Almost all soups can be made in advance. Many, in fact, are better on the second or third day, after the flavors have mingled.

Creamy Turkey Soup

3 (14 ounce) cans chicken broth	3 (396 g)
1 pound russet potatoes, peeled, cubed	.5 kg
3 ribs celery, sliced	
1 (15 ounce) can sliced carrots, drained	425 g
1 (10 ounce) package frozen yellow squash	280 g
2 teaspoons minced garlic	10 ml
1 teaspoon dried thyme	5 ml
1½ cups cooked, shredded turkey	360 ml
1 (10 ounce) can cream of chicken soup	280 g
1 cup milk or half-and-half cream	240 ml

- Combine chicken broth, ½ cup (120 ml) water, potatoes and celery in soup pot and boil. Add salt and pepper to taste and cook on medium heat about 20 minutes or until potatoes and celery are tender. Add carrots, squash, garlic and thyme and cook another 10 minutes.

- Stir in shredded turkey, chicken soup and milk and heat just until soup is thoroughly hot, but do not boil.

Turkey With Avocado

3 large potatoes, peeled, cubed
2 (14 ounce) cans chicken broth   2 (396 g)
1 teaspoon ground thyme   5 ml
½ pound smoked turkey breast, cubed   227 g
1 (10 ounce) package frozen corn   280 g
3 slices bacon, cooked crisp, drained
1 large avocado
4 plum tomatoes, coarsely chopped
1 lime

- Combine potatoes, broth and thyme in pot, cover and boil. Reduce heat and simmer until potatoes are tender, about 15 minutes.

- With slotted spoon transfer half of potatoes to blender or food processor, puree and pour into soup pot. Add turkey, remaining potatoes and corn and simmer for 5 minutes.

- Crumble bacon, peel and slice avocado. Add bacon, avocado, tomatoes, juice of lime and salt and pepper to taste to turkey mixture and stir gently to mix.

TIP: Peel and cut avocado just before serving, because they turn dark so quickly.

Use frozen vegetables such as peas, spinach or corn to cut prep time. Add them to assorted soups or puree them with broth, cream and sauteed onion, then simmer to make a smooth soup.

Last-Minute Turkey Help

2 (14 ounce) cans chicken broth	2 (396 g)
1 small zucchini, sliced	
1 (16 ounce) package frozen vegetable and	
pasta mix	.5 kg
1½ cups cooked, cubed turkey	360 ml
4 fresh green onions, sliced	

- Combine broth, ¼ cup (60 ml) water, zucchini, vegetable mix and cubed turkey in large saucepan.

- Boil, reduce heat and simmer for 10 to 12 minutes or until vegetables and pasta are tender. Garnish each serving with sliced green onions before serving.

Tasty Turkey-Veggie Soup

2 (14 ounce) cans chicken broth	2 (396 g)
2 teaspoons minced garlic	10 ml
1 (16 ounce) package frozen corn	.5 kg
1 (10 ounce) package frozen cut green beans	280 g
1 (10 ounce) package frozen sliced carrots	280 g
2 (15 ounce) cans stewed tomatoes	2 (425 g)
2½ cups cooked, cubed turkey	600 ml
1 cup shredded mozzarella cheese	240 ml

- Combine broth, 1 cup (240 ml) water, garlic, corn, green beans, carrots, tomatoes, turkey and 1 teaspoon (5 ml) salt in large, heavy soup pot.

- Boil, reduce heat and simmer for 15 minutes. Before serving, top each bowl of soup with mozzarella cheese.

So Easy, Creamy Turkey Soup

1 (10 ounce) can cream of celery soup	280 g
1 (10 ounce) can cream of chicken soup	280 g
1 soup can milk	
1 cup finely diced turkey	240 ml

• Combine all ingredients in large saucepan. Serve hot.

Hearty 15-Minute Turkey Soup

This is great served with cornbread.

1 (14 ounce) can chicken broth	396 g
3 (15 ounce) cans navy beans with liquid	3 425 g)
1 (28 ounce) can stewed tomatoes with liquid	794 g
3 cups cooked, cubed white turkey	710 ml
2 teaspoons minced garlic	10 ml
¼ teaspoon cayenne pepper	1 ml
1 (6 ounce) package baby spinach,	
stems removed	168 g

• Combine broth, beans, stewed tomatoes, turkey, garlic, cayenne pepper and salt and pepper to taste in soup pot. Boil, reduce heat and simmer on medium heat for about 10 minutes.

• Stir in baby spinach, boil and cook, stirring constantly, for 5 minutes.

Fast Gobbler Fix

1 (16 ounce) package frozen chopped onions and bell peppers	.5 kg
2 (3 ounce) packages chicken-flavored ramen noodles	2 (84 g)
2 (10 ounce) cans cream of chicken soup	2 (280 g)
1 cup cooked, cubed turkey	240 ml

- Cook onions and peppers in soup pot with a little oil just until tender but not brown. Add ramen noodles with seasoning packet and 4 cups (1 L) water. Cook for 5 minutes or until noodles are tender. Stir in chicken soup and cubed turkey. Heat, stirring constantly, until thoroughly hot.

Turkey Tango

This is spicy, but not too spicy. It's just right! Try it with chicken too.

3 - 4 cups chopped turkey	710 ml
2 (14 ounce) cans condensed chicken broth	2 (396 g)
2 (10 ounce) cans diced tomatoes and green chilies	2 (280 g)
1 (15 ounce) can whole corn, drained	425 g
1 large onion, chopped	
1 (10 ounce) can tomato soup	280 g
1 teaspoon garlic powder	5 ml
1 teaspoon dried oregano	5 ml
3 tablespoons cornstarch	45 ml

- Combine turkey, broth, tomatoes and green chilies, corn, onion, tomato soup, garlic powder and oregano in large roasting pan. Mix cornstarch with 3 tablespoons (45 ml) water and add to soup mixture. Bring mixture to boil, reduce heat and simmer for 2 hours. Stir occasionally.

Smoked Turkey-Sausage Soup

2 tablespoons oil	30 ml
1 small onion, chopped	
1 green bell pepper, seeded, chopped	
1 (14 ounce) can chicken broth	396 g
1 medium potato, peeled, cubed	
½ teaspoon dried basil	2 ml
1 pound smoked turkey kielbasa, sliced	.5 kg
1 (15 ounce) can great northern beans	
with liquid	425 g

- Combine oil, onion and bell pepper in soup pot and cook for 5 minutes. Stir in broth, potato, basil, turkey kielbasa, 1 cup (240 ml) water and salt and pepper to taste. Boil, reduce heat to medium and simmer for 15 minutes or until potato is tender. Stir in beans and heat until thoroughly hot.

Turkey Tenders Gobble

½ cup uncooked wild rice	120 ml
3 ribs celery, sliced	
1 onion, chopped	
1 (4 ounce) can sliced mushrooms, drained	114 g
¼ cup (½ stick) butter	60 ml
2 (14 ounce) cans chicken broth	2 (396g)
1 ½ pounds turkey tenderloins	.7 kg
1 (15 ounce) can stewed tomatoes	425 g

- Mix all ingredients with ½ cup (120 ml) water in soup pot and bring to boil. Reduce heat and simmer for 45 to 55 minutes or until wild rice is tender.

- Remove turkey tenderloins with slotted spoon, cut into bite-size pieces and add to soup mixture. Heat until thoroughly hot and serve.

Turkey and Rice Soup

¼ cup (½ stick) butter	60 ml
1 onion, chopped	
3 ribs celery, finely chopped	
1 bell pepper, seeded, chopped	
2 (14 ounce) cans turkey broth	2 (396 g)
1 (6 ounce) box roasted-garlic long grain, wild rice	168 g
2 (10 ounce) cans cream of chicken soup	2 (280 g)
2 cups cooked, diced white meat turkey	480 ml
1 cup milk	240 ml

- Melt butter in soup pot over medium heat. Add onion, celery and bell pepper and cook for 10 minutes. Add turkey broth, 1 ½ cups (360 ml) water and rice and boil. Reduce heat and cook on low for about 15 minutes or until rice is tender.

- Stir in chicken soup, turkey, milk and ¾ teaspoon (4 ml) pepper. Stir constantly and cook on medium heat until mixture is thoroughly hot.

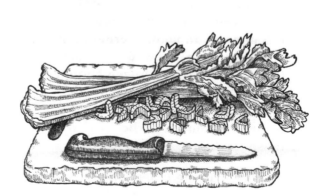

Turkey-Chili Supper

1 onion, finely chopped	
2 (15 ounce) cans navy beans	2 (425 g)
2 (14 ounce) cans chicken broth	2 (396 g)
1 (7 ounce) can diced green chilies	198 g
2 teaspoons ground cumin	10 ml
1 teaspoon dried oregano	5 ml
¼ teaspoon cayenne pepper	1 ml
4 cups cooked, cubed turkey	1 L
1 (12 ounce) package shredded Monterey Jack cheese, divided	340 g

- Combine all ingredients except cheese in soup pot and boil. Reduce heat and simmer for 20 minutes.

- Just before serving, stir in about 2 cups (480 ml) cheese and stir constantly. Ladle into individual soup bowls and sprinkle remaining cheese on top.

Creole Turkey Gumbo

1 (32 ounce) carton chicken broth	1 kg
1 pound cooked turkey, cubed	.5 kg
1 (15 ounce) can whole kernel corn	425 g
2 (15 ounce) cans stewed tomatoes	2 (425 g)
1 (10 ounce) package frozen chopped okra, thawed	280 g
¾ cup instant rice	180 ml
2 teaspoons minced garlic	10 ml
1 teaspoon Creole seasoning	5 ml

- Combine all ingredients in large soup pot and bring to boil. Reduce heat and simmer for 15 minutes.

Big Bold Beefy Bowls

Fresh Beefy Vegetable Soup

1 pound lean ground beef	.5 kg
1 onion, chopped	
1 (15 ounce) can Italian stewed tomatoes	425 g
1 cup freshly cut corn	240 ml
1 large potato, peeled, cubed	
3 ribs celery, sliced	
1 carrot, thinly sliced	
1 cup fresh green peas or lima beans	240 ml
1 teaspoon dried Italian seasoning	5 ml
½ teaspoon hot sauce	2 ml
2 (14 ounce) cans beef broth	2 (396 g)
2 tablespoons flour	30 ml

- Brown beef and onion in large, heavy soup pot over medium heat. Add stewed tomatoes, corn, potato, celery, carrot, peas or beans, Italian seasoning, hot sauce, beef broth and 2 cups (480 ml) water. Boil, reduce heat and simmer for 1 hour.

- Combine flour and ¼ cup (60 ml) water and stir to make paste. On medium heat, add paste to soup with salt and pepper to taste and cook, stirring constantly, until soup thickens.

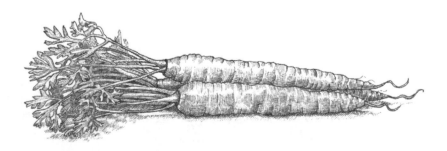

Speedy Vegetable Soup

1 pound lean ground beef	.5 kg
2 (15 ounce) cans stewed tomatoes	2 (425 g)
3 (14 ounce) cans beef broth	3 (396 g)
1 (16 ounce) package frozen mixed vegetables	.5 kg
½ cup instant brown rice	120 ml

- Brown ground beef in skillet, cook and stir until beef crumbles. Transfer to soup pot and add tomatoes, beef broth and vegetables.

- Boil, reduce heat and simmer for 20 minutes, stirring occasionally. Add brown rice and cook on medium heat for 5 minutes.

Beefy Veggie Soup

1 pound lean ground beef	.5 kg
1 (46 ounce) can cocktail vegetable juice	1.3 kg
1 (1 ounce) packet onion soup mix	28 g
1 (3 ounce) package beef-flavored ramen noodles	84 g
1 (16 ounce) package frozen mixed vegetables	.5 kg

- Cook beef until no longer pink in large soup pot over medium heat. Drain. Stir in cocktail juice, soup mix, seasoning packet in noodles and mixed vegetables.

- Heat mixture to boiling, reduce heat and simmer uncovered for 6 minutes or until vegetables are tender-crisp. Boil again, stir in noodles and cook for 3 minutes.

Franks and Veggie Soup

¼ cup (½ stick) butter	60 ml
2 onions, finely chopped	
1 red bell pepper, seeded, chopped	
2 teaspoons minced garlic	10 ml
1 (28 ounce) can baked beans	794 g
1 (10 ounce) package frozen mixed vegetables	280 g
1 (14 ounce) can beef broth	396 g
6 frankfurters, cut into 1-inch slices	2.5 cm
1 tablespoon Worcestershire sauce	15 ml
1 cup shredded colby cheese	240 ml

- Melt butter in large saucepan over medium heat and cook onions, bell pepper and garlic for 5 minutes.

- Stir in beans, mixed vegetables, broth, frankfurters, 1 cup (240 ml) water and Worcestershire. Cook over medium heat, 5 minutes and stir occasionally.

- Ladle into individual soup bowls and sprinkle each serving with cheese.

Former U.S. presidents have all shared a love of soup. George H.W. Bush preferred New England clam chowder, while John F. Kennedy loved the fish chowder of his childhood. Bill Clinton and Dwight Eisenhower liked vegetable beef soup.

Mother's Beef-Veggie Soup

1 pound lean ground beef	.5 kg
1 (1 ounce) packet onion soup mix	28 g
2 (14 ounce) cans beef broth	2 (396g)
2 (15 ounce) cans stewed tomatoes	2 (425 g)
2 (15 ounce) cans mixed vegetables with liquid	2 (425 g)
1 cup shell macaroni	240 ml

- Brown beef in soup pot over high heat and drain. Reduce heat to medium and add soup mix, broth, tomatoes, mixed vegetables and 1 cup (240 ml) water and cook for 5 minutes.

- Stir in macaroni and cook for 15 minutes or until macaroni is tender, stirring occasionally.

Down-Home Beefy Soup

1 ½ pounds lean ground beef	.7 kg
1 (16 ounce) package frozen onions and peppers	.5 kg
2 teaspoons minced garlic	10 ml
2 (14 ounce) cans beef broth	2 (396 g)
2 (15 ounce) cans Italian stewed tomatoes	2 (425 g)
3 teaspoons Italian seasoning	15 ml
1 ½ cups macaroni	360 ml
Shredded cheddar cheese	

- On medium heat, brown and cook beef, onions and peppers and garlic in soup pot. Add beef broth, 2 cups (480 ml) water, stewed tomatoes and Italian seasoning and boil 2 minutes.

- Add macaroni and cook, stirring occasionally, on medium heat for about 15 minutes. When serving, sprinkle cheese over each serving.

Vegetable-Beef Soup

1 ½ pounds lean ground beef	.7 kg
3 (15 ounce) cans mixed vegetables with liquid	3 (425 g)
1 (1 ounce) packet onion soup mix	28 g
1 (48 ounce) can cocktail vegetable juice	1.3 kg
1 (14 ounce) can beef broth	396 g
½ cup barley	120 ml

- Brown ground beef in roasting pan, stir to crumble and drain. Add all remaining ingredients with 1 cup (240 ml) water, boil and simmer 15 minutes.

Italian Vegetable Soup

1 pound lean ground beef	.5 kg
2 teaspoons minced garlic	10 ml
1 green bell pepper, seeded, chopped	
2 (14 ounce) cans beef broth	2 (396 g)
1 (15 ounce) can Italian stewed tomatoes	425 g
2 small zucchini, sliced	
1 (15 ounce) can cannellini beans, rinsed, drained	425 g
1 (10 ounce) package frozen chopped spinach, thawed	280 g

- Brown and cook beef and garlic in soup pot for 5 minutes or until beef crumbles. Stir in bell pepper, broth, tomatoes, zucchini and beans and cook on medium heat for 15 minutes.

- Add spinach and continue cooking another 10 minutes.

No-Brainer Heidelberg Soup

2 (10 ounce) cans potato soup   2 (280 g)
1 (10 ounce) can cream of celery soup   280 g
1 soup can milk
6 slices salami, chopped
10 green onions, chopped

- Cook potato soup, celery soup and milk in large saucepan on medium heat, stirring constantly, just until thoroughly hot.

- Saute salami and onions in well greased skillet and add to soup.

- Heat thoroughly and serve hot.

Italian Beefy Veggie Soup

1 pound lean ground beef   .5 kg
2 teaspoons minced garlic   10 ml
2 (15 ounce) cans Italian stewed tomatoes   2 (425 g)
2 (14 ounce) cans beef broth   2 (396 g)
2 teaspoons Italian seasoning   10 ml
1 (16 ounce) package frozen mixed vegetables   .5 kg
⅓ cup shell macaroni   80 ml
1 (8 ounce) package shredded Italian cheese   227 g

- Cook beef and garlic in large soup pot for 5 minutes. Stir in tomatoes, broth, 1 cup (240 ml) water, seasoning, mixed vegetables, macaroni and salt and pepper to taste.

- Boil, reduce heat and simmer for 10 to 15 minutes or until macaroni is tender.

- Ladle into individual serving bowls and sprinkle several tablespoons cheese over top of soup.

Easy Mexican Beef Soup

2 pounds lean ground beef	1 kg
2 (15 ounce) cans chili without beans	2 (425 g)
3 (14 ounce) cans beef broth	3 (396 g)
2 (15 ounce) cans Mexican stewed tomatoes	2 (425 g)
2 (4 ounce) cans diced green chilies	2 (114 g)

- Brown ground beef until no longer pink in skillet and transfer to soup pot.

- Add chili, broth, stewed tomatoes, green chilies, 1 cup (240 ml) water, 1 teaspoon (5 ml) salt and stir well.

- Cover and cook on low to medium for about 45 minutes.

Southwestern Soup

1 ½ pounds lean ground beef	.7 kg
1 large onion, chopped	
2 (15 ounce) cans pinto beans with liquid	2 (425 g)
1 (15 ounce) can ranch-style beans, drained	425 g
2 (15 ounce) cans whole kernel corn with liquid	2 (425 g)
2 (15 ounce) cans Mexican stewed tomatoes	2 (425 g)
2 (1 ounce) packets taco seasoning	2 (28 g)

- Brown beef and onion in large soup pot, stir until beef crumbles and drain. Add beans, corn, tomatoes and 1 ½ cups (360 ml) water.

- Boil, reduce heat and stir in taco seasoning. Simmer for 25 minutes.

Kitchen-Sink Taco Soup

1 ¼ pounds lean ground beef	567 g
1 onion, chopped	
1 (1 ounce) packet ranch dressing mix	28 g
2 (15 ounce) cans pinto beans with liquid	2 (425 g)
1 (15 ounce) can whole kernel corn with liquid	425 g
1 (15 ounce) can cream-style corn	425 g
3 (15 ounce) cans Mexican stewed tomatoes with liquid	3 (425 g)
Tortilla chips	
1 (8 ounce) package shredded Monterey Jack cheese	227 g

- Brown ground beef and onion in skillet, drain and stir in ranch dressing mix.

- Combine beef-onion mixture, beans, corn, cream-style corn and stewed tomatoes in roasting pan.

- Boil, lower heat and simmer for 10 to 15 minutes. Serve over tortilla chips and sprinkle with cheese.

Cantina Taco Soup

1 ½ pounds lean ground beef	.7 kg
1 (1 ounce) packet taco seasoning	28 g
2 (15 ounce) cans Mexican stewed tomatoes	2 (425 g)
1 (15 ounce) can whole kernel corn, drained	425 g
Crushed tortilla chips	
Shredded cheddar cheese	

- Brown ground beef in skillet until it is no longer pink and transfer to soup pot. Add taco seasoning, tomatoes, corn and 1 cup (240 ml) water.

- On high heat, boil, reduce heat and simmer for about 35 minutes.

- When serving, spoon 1 heaping tablespoon (15 ml) crushed tortilla chips and 1 heaping tablespoon (15 ml) cheese over each serving.

Quick Enchilada Soup

1 pound lean ground beef, browned, drained	.5 kg
1 (15 ounce) can Mexican stewed tomatoes	425 g
2 (15 ounce) cans pinto beans with liquid	2 (425 g)
1 (15 ounce) can whole kernel corn with liquid	425 g
1 onion, chopped	
2 (10 ounce) cans enchilada sauce	2 (280 g)
1 (8 ounce) package shredded 4-cheese blend	227 g

- Combine beef, tomatoes, beans, corn, onion, enchilada sauce and 1 cup (240 ml) water in soup pot.

- Boil, reduce heat and simmer for 35 minutes. When serving, sprinkle a little shredded cheese over each serving.

Across-the-Border Tamale Soup

1 pound lean ground beef	.5 kg
1 (16 ounce) package frozen chopped onions and bell peppers	.5 kg
2 tablespoons oil	30 ml
1 (10 ounce) package frozen corn	280 g
2 (14 ounce) cans beef broth	2 (396 g)
1 (15 ounce) can pinto beans with liquid	425 g
2 tablespoons chili powder	30 ml
1 teaspoon ground cumin	5 ml
1 (28 ounce) can tamales with liquid, shucked, quartered	794 g

- In large skillet, brown beef, onions and bell peppers in oil.

- Transfer to soup pot and add corn, broth, beans, chili powder, cumin and salt and pepper to taste.

- Boil, reduce heat and simmer for 30 minutes. About 15 minutes prior to serving, add tamale chunks and heat thoroughly. Stir gently so tamales will not break. Serve hot.

TIP: For a spicier soup, you could add 1 (10 ounce/280g) can tomatoes and green chilies.

Albondigas Soup

This is a very traditional meatball-potato soup.

2 pounds lean ground beef	1 kg
1 cup breadcrumbs	240 ml
1 onion, chopped	
2 eggs	
2 teaspoons cumin	10 ml
2 cloves garlic, minced	
4 tablespoons bacon drippings or butter	60 ml
2 tablespoons flour	30 ml
3 tablespoons snipped cilantro	45 ml
2 large potatoes, cubed	

- Combine beef, breadcrumbs, onion, eggs, cumin and garlic with 1 teaspoon (5 ml) salt and ½ teaspoon (2 ml) pepper. Mix well and form into meatballs about 1 ¼ inches (2.5 cm) in diameter. Brown meatballs on all sides in large skillet. Transfer to bowl and set aside.

- Heat bacon drippings or butter in same skillet and sprinkle flour on top. Stir constantly until flour browns. (Do not burn.)

- Add 4 cups (1 L) hot water, cilantro and ½ teaspoon (2 ml) salt and continue to stir until liquid boils. Add potatoes and meatballs and simmer until potatoes are done.

Easy Meaty Minestrone

2 (20 ounce) cans minestrone soup	2 (567 g)
1 (15 ounce) can pinto beans with liquid	425 g
1 (18 ounce) package frozen Italian meatballs, thawed	510 g
1 (5 ounce) package grated parmesan cheese	143 g

- Combine soups, beans, meatballs and ½ cup (120 ml) water in large saucepan. Boil, reduce heat and simmer for about 15 minutes.

- To serve, sprinkle each serving with parmesan cheese.

Spaghetti Soup

1 (7 ounce) package pre-cut spaghetti	198 g
1 (18 ounce) package frozen, cooked meatballs, thawed	510 g
1 (28 ounce) jar spaghetti sauce	794 g
1 (15 ounce) can Mexican stewed tomatoes	425 g

- Cook spaghetti in soup pot with 2 quarts (2 L) boiling water and a little salt about 6 minutes (no need to drain).

- When spaghetti is done, add meatballs, spaghetti sauce and stewed tomatoes and cook until mixture heats through.

TIP: If you want to garnish each soup bowl, sprinkle with 2 tablespoons (30 ml) mozzarella cheese or whatever cheese you have in the refrigerator.

Chunky Beefy Noodle Soup

1 pound beef round steak, cubed	.5 kg
1 onion, chopped	
2 ribs celery, sliced	
1 tablespoon oil	15 ml
1 tablespoon chili powder	15 ml
½ teaspoon dried oregano	2 ml
1 (15 ounce) can stewed tomatoes	425 g
2 (14 ounce) cans beef broth	2 (396 g)
½ (8 ounce) package uncooked egg noodles	½ (227 g)
1 green bell pepper, seeded, chopped	

- Cook and stir cubed steak, onion and celery in soup pot with oil for 15 minutes or until beef browns.

- Stir in 2 cups (480 ml) water, 1 teaspoon (5 ml) salt, chili powder, oregano, stewed tomatoes and beef broth. Boil, reduce heat and simmer 1½ to 2 hours or until beef is tender.

- Stir in noodles and green pepper and heat to boiling. Reduce heat and simmer 10 to 15 minutes or until noodles are tender.

Savory soups and stews often taste better if made a day or two in advance and reheated just before serving.

Quick Beef-Veggie Soup

1 pound round steak, cubed	.5 kg
2 (15 ounce) cans beef broth	2 (396 g)
1 (6 ounce) can tomato sauce	168 g
1 (15 ounce) can Mexican stewed tomatoes	425 g
1 (15 ounce) can mixed vegetables with liquid	425 g
1 (8 ounce) can whole kernel corn, drained	227 g

- Brown steak on medium heat in soup pot for 10 minutes. Add beef broth and tomato sauce and simmer for 15 minutes.

- Stir in stewed tomatoes, mixed vegetables and corn and cook another 10 minutes.

Meatball Soup

1 (18 ounce) package frozen, cooked Italian meatballs	510 g
2 (14 ounce) cans beef broth	2 (396 g)
2 (15 ounce) cans Italian stewed tomatoes	2 (425 g)
1 (16 ounce) package frozen stew vegetables	.5 kg

- Place meatballs, beef broth and stewed tomatoes in large saucepan. Boil, reduce heat and simmer for 10 minutes or until meatballs are thoroughly hot.

- Add vegetables and cook on medium heat for 10 minutes.

  TIP: If you like your soup thicker, mix 2 tablespoons (30 ml) cornstarch in ¼ cup (60 ml) water and stir into soup, bring to boiling and stir constantly until soup thickens.

Steak Soup

1 pound ground sirloin steak	.5 kg
2 (10 ounce) cans vegetable soup	2 (280 g)
2 (10 ounce) cans tomatoes and green chilies	2 (280 g)

- Brown ground sirloin in skillet, crumble and drain.

- Stir in soups, tomatoes and green chilies with juice.

- Heat on medium to low for 15 to 20 minutes or until hot. Stir often.

Black Bean-Barbecue Soup

1 onion, finely chopped	
2 tablespoons olive oil	30 ml
2 teaspoons minced garlic	10 ml
2 (14 ounce) cans chicken broth	2 (396 g)
3 (15 ounce) cans black beans, rinsed, drained	3 (425 g)
1 (10 ounce) can diced tomatoes and	
green chilies	280 g
1 pound shredded barbecue beef	.5 kg
2 tablespoons red wine vinegar	30 ml
Shredded Monterey Jack cheese	

- Saute onion in oil in soup pot over medium heat, stir in garlic and saute 1 more minute. Stir in broth, beans and tomatoes and green chilies. Reduce heat and simmer, stirring often, for 15 minutes.

- Process 1 cup (240 ml) bean mixture in food processor until smooth. Return puree to soup pot, add beef and simmer for 10 minutes. Stir in vinegar and garnish each bowl with cheese.

Menudo

*This could also be called **Mexican Hangover Helper** or at least it is reported to be a sure cure for the morning after.*

2 pounds tripe	**1 kg**
1 bunch green onions with tops, chopped	
3 cloves garlic, minced	
¾ cup snipped fresh cilantro leaves, divided	**180 ml**
Fresh lime slices	

- Wash tripe very well and dry with paper towels. Place tripe in soup pot with enough water to cover plus 3 inches (8 cm).

- Add onions and garlic, boil, reduce heat and simmer for 6 to 8 hours until tripe is tender. Add water if necessary.

- When tripe is tender, remove from pot and cool about 15 minutes. Cut into small pieces and return to soup pot.

- Add ¼ cup (60 ml) cilantro and cook another 1 to 2 hours. Serve in large soup bowls and garnish with cilantro and lime slices.

  *TIP: **Menudo** or tripe soup is a favorite in Mexico. Tripe is the inner lining of beef stomach, is very tough and requires long cooking times.*

Blue Norther Stew

Cold fronts in the south are called northers. This is a great choice for one of those cold, winter days.

1 ½ pounds lean ground beef	.7 kg
1 onion, chopped	
1 (1 ounce) packet taco seasoning	28 g
1 (1 ounce) packet ranch dressing mix	28 g
1 (15 ounce) can whole kernel corn, drained	425 g
1 (15 ounce) can kidney beans with liquid	425 g
2 (15 ounce) cans pinto beans	2 (425 g
2 (15 ounce) cans Mexican stewed tomatoes	2 (425 g)
1 (10 ounce) can tomatoes and green chilies	280 g

- Brown ground beef and onion in large roasting pan. Add both packets seasonings and mix well.

- Add corn, beans, stewed tomatoes, tomatoes and green chilies and 1 cup (240 ml) water, mix well and simmer for about 30 minutes.

Vegetable-Beef Stew

1 pound stew meat	.5 kg
1 (14 ounce) can beef broth	396 g
1 (28 ounce) can stewed tomatoes	794 g
2 (15 ounce) cans mixed vegetables with liquid	2 (425 g)
½ cup barley	120 ml

- Combine meat, broth and 2 cups (240 ml) water and salt and pepper to taste in large stew pot, boil. Reduce heat to low and cook for 1 hour. Stir in all remaining ingredients and cook on medium heat for 30 minutes.

Bronco Stew

2 pounds ground round beef	1 kg
1 (16 ounce) package frozen, chopped onions and bell peppers	.5 kg
1 (14 ounce) can beef broth	396 g
1 (1 ounce) packet taco seasoning	28 g
2 (15 ounce) cans Mexican stewed tomatoes	2 (425 g)
2 (15 ounce) cans pinto beans with jalapenos	2 (425 g)
1 (16 ounce) package cubed processed cheese	.5 kg
1 (13 ounce) package tortilla chips, crushed	370 g

- In stew pot, brown beef on all sides in a little oil on high heat and stir often. Add onion and bell peppers and cook 3 minutes. Add broth and taco seasoning, reduce heat and simmer 35 to 45 minutes or until most of liquid has evaporated. Stir in tomatoes and beans and heat just until mixture is thoroughly hot. Add cheese and stir until cheese melts.

- Place about ¾ cup (180 ml) of crushed chips in bottom of individual soup bowls and spoon stew over chips and serve immediately.

Minute Stew

1 pound extra-lean ground beef	.5 kg
1 (14 ounce) can beef broth	396 g
1 (15 ounce) can stewed tomatoes with onions	425 g
1 (8 ounce) can whole kernel corn, drained	227 g
1 (15 ounce) can mixed vegetables	425 g

- Brown ground meat in skillet and drain.

- Add broth, tomatoes, corn and vegetables to skillet and mix well.

- Simmer for 20 to 30 minutes and stir often.

Quick Brunswick Stew

Brunswick Stew is a favorite in Virginia and other southern states. The original version takes all day to make, but this is a quick substitute that is great in a pinch.

1 (15 ounce) can beef stew	425 g
1 (15 ounce) can chicken stew	425 g
1 (15 ounce) can lima beans with liquid	425 g
2 (15 ounce) cans stewed tomatoes with liquid	2 (425 g)
1 (15 ounce) can whole kernel corn	425 g
½ teaspoon hot sauce	2 ml

- Combine beef stew, chicken stew, beans, tomatoes and corn in large stew pot. On medium heat, bring to a boil, reduce heat and simmer for 20 minutes.

- Brunswick Stew needs to be a little spicy, so stir in ¼ teaspoon (1 ml) hot sauce at first, taste and add more if needed. If you don't want spicy, add 1 tablespoon (15 ml) Worcestershire sauce to stew. It is best served with hot cornbread muffins.

Baked Pinto Bean Stew

1 cup dried pinto beans	240 ml
1 pound beef stew meat	.5 kg
1 onion, chopped	
1 (6 ounce) can tomato paste	227 g
¼ cup packed brown sugar	60 ml
½ teaspoon dry mustard	2 ml
¼ teaspoon ground cinnamon	1 ml

- Preheat oven to 325° (162° C). Place beans in Dutch oven and add 5 cups (1.3 L) water and boil for 2 minutes.

- Add remaining ingredients with salt and pepper to taste. Cover and bake 2 hours.

Stroganoff Stew

1 (1 ounce) packet dry onion soup mix	28 g
2 (10 ounce) cans golden mushroom soup	2 (280 g)
2 pounds stew meat	1 kg
1 (8 ounce) carton sour cream	227 g
Hot, cooked noodles	

- Combine soup mix, mushroom soup and 2 soup cans water and pour over stew meat in roasting pan.

- Cover tightly and bake at 275° (135° C) for 6 to 8 hours.

- When ready to serve, stir in sour cream, return mixture to oven until it heats thoroughly and serve over noodles.

Meat and Potato Stew

2 pounds beef stew meat	1 kg
2 (15 ounce) cans new potatoes, drained	2 (425 g)
1 (15 ounce) can sliced carrots, drained	425 g
2 (10 ounce) cans French onion soup	2 (280 g)

- Season meat with salt and pepper and cook with 2 cups (480 ml) water in large pot for 1 hour. Add potatoes, carrots and onion soup and mix well.

- Boil, reduce heat and simmer for 30 minutes.

Oven-Baked Beef Stew

1 tablespoon flour	15 ml
¾ pound beef chuck, cubed	340 g
¾ cup chopped onion	180 ml
¼ teaspoon basil	1 ml
2 potatoes, peeled, cubed	
2 carrots, peeled, sliced	
¼ cup dry red wine	60 ml
1 (10 ounce) can tomato soup	280 g

- Combine flour with salt and pepper and pat onto both sides of meat. Brown meat in large iron skillet. Transfer to large, deep skillet.

- Add all remaining ingredients with 1¼ cups (300 ml) water; cover and bake at 325° (162° C) for about 1 hour.

Pirate Stew For The Crew

If you can open cans, you can make this stew. Don't let the number of ingredients get to you. Leave something out if you get tired of opening cans, but by all means, you can handle this recipe.

3 pounds beef chuck roast, cubed	1.3 kg
2 (15 ounce) cans diced tomatoes	2 (425 g)
2 (32 ounce) cans V-8 juice	2 (1 kg)
2 (15 ounce) cans green beans, drained	2 (425 g)
2 (15 ounce) cans field peas with snaps, drained	2 (425 g)
2 (15 ounce) cans green peas, drained	2 (425 g)
2 (14 ounce) cans cut okra, drained	2 (396 g)
2 (16 ounce) packages frozen lima beans	2 (.5 kg)
2 (16 ounce) packages frozen yellow corn	2 (.5 kg)
1 (16 ounce) package frozen white corn	.5 kg
2 pounds onion, peeled, diced	1 kg
4 pounds potatoes, peeled, cubed	1.8 kg
1 teaspoon dried rosemary	5 ml

- Brown roast in oil in bottom of large stew pot. Add vegetables with 1-quart (1 L) water and season with salt, pepper and rosemary.

- Simmer all day. Remove excess fat before serving.

  TIP: This recipe makes enough for several meals so freeze some for later.

Here's a great idea for serving a hearty soup: slice the top from a big, chunky round loaf of bread, lightly toast the loaf and fill it with soup for an edible bowl (and easy clean-up).

Blue Ribbon Beef Stew

1 (2 ½ pound) boneless beef chuck roast, cubed	1.2 kg
⅓ cup flour	80 ml
2 (14 ounce) cans beef broth	2 (396 g)
1 teaspoon dried thyme	5 ml
2 teaspoons minced garlic	10 ml
1 pound new, red potatoes with peel, sliced	.5 kg
2 large carrots, sliced	
3 ribs celery, sliced	
2 onions, finely chopped	
1 (10 ounce) package frozen green peas	280 g

- Dredge beef in flour and 1 teaspoon (5 ml) salt; reserve leftover flour. Brown half beef in stew pot over medium heat for about 10 minutes, transfer to plate.

- Repeat with remaining beef. Add reserved flour to stew pot and cook, stirring constantly, for 1 minute.

- Stir in beef broth, ½ cup (120 ml) water, thyme and garlic and boil. Reduce heat and simmer for 50 minutes and stir occasionally.

- Add potatoes, carrots, celery and onion and cook for 30 minutes. Stir in green peas, salt and pepper to taste, heat to boiling. Serve hot.

Border-Crossing Stew

1 ½ pounds round steak, cubed	.7 kg
2 onions, chopped	
1 (14 ounce) can beef broth	396 g
1 (15 ounce) can Mexican stewed tomatoes	425 g
1 (7 ounce) can chopped green chilies	198 g
3 baking potatoes, peeled, cubed	
2 teaspoons minced garlic	10 ml
2 teaspoons ground cumin	10 ml

- Brown and cook cubed steak and onion in stew pot for 10 minutes and stir often.

- Mix in beef broth, tomatoes, green chilies, potatoes, garlic, cumin, 1 cup (240 ml) water, salt and pepper to taste. Cover and cook on low to medium heat for 35 minutes or until potatoes are tender.

Steakhouse Stew

1 pound boneless beef sirloin steak, cubed	.5 kg
1 (15 ounce) can stewed tomatoes	425 g
1 (10 ounce) can French onion soup	280 g
1 (10 ounce) can tomato soup	280 g
1 (16 ounce) package frozen stew vegetables, thawed	.5 kg

- Cook steak in skillet with a little oil until juices evaporate. Transfer to stew pot or roasting pan.

- Add 1 cup (240 ml) water, tomatoes, soups and vegetables and heat to boiling. Reduce heat to low and simmer 35 minutes.

Green Chile Stew Pot Caldillo

Caldillo or stew is a traditional Mexican dish served on special occasions.

2 pounds round steak, cubed	**1 kg**
Canola oil	
2 onions, chopped	
2 potatoes, peeled, diced	
2 cloves garlic, minced	
6 - 8 fresh green chilies, roasted, peeled, seeded, diced	

- Sprinkle round steak with 1 tablespoon (15 ml) salt; heat oil in large skillet and brown meat. Put onions, potatoes and garlic in same skillet and cook until onions are translucent.

- Pour all ingredients from skillet into large stew pot. Add chilies, 1 teaspoon (5 ml) salt and ½ teaspoon (2 ml) pepper and enough water to cover. Boil, lower heat and simmer for 1 to 2 hours or until meat and potatoes are tender.

Did you know ice cubes love fat? Eliminate fat from soup by dropping ice cubes into your soup pot. As you stir, the fat will cling to the cubes.

Cattle Drive Chili Stew

3 pounds stew meat	1.3 kg
3 tablespoons oil	45 ml
1 medium onion, chopped	
3 ribs celery, chopped	
2 (15 ounce) cans Mexican stewed tomatoes with liquid	2 (425 g)
2 (14 ounce) cans beef broth	2 (396 g)
1 (10 ounce) package frozen whole kernel corn	280 g
1 cup diced, fresh green chilies	240 ml

- Brown stew meat on all sides in large skillet with oil and transfer to large stew pot. In skillet drippings, saute onion and celery until translucent and pour drippings and vegetables into stew pot.

- Stir in tomatoes, beef broth, corn, chilies, 2 teaspoons (10 ml) salt and ¼ teaspoon (1 ml) pepper and boil. Reduce heat and simmer several hours.

   TIP: If soup is too thin, add ¼ cup (60 ml) instant mashed potato flakes.

Chili-Soup Warmer

1 (10 ounce) can tomato-bisque soup	280 g
1 (10 ounce) can fiesta chili-beef soup	280 g
1 (10 ounce) can chili	280 g
1(14 ounce) can beef broth	396 g

- Combine soups, chili and broth in saucepan. Add amount of water to produce desired thickness of soup.

- Heat and serve hot with crackers.

Cadillac Chili

Oil	
1 ½ pounds lean ground beef	.7 kg
2 pounds chili ground beef	1 kg
1 onion, chopped	
1 (15 ounce) can tomato sauce	425 g
1 (10 ounce) can diced tomatoes and green chilies	280 g
4 tablespoons ground cumin	60 ml
1 teaspoon oregano	5 ml
2 tablespoons chili powder	30 ml
1 (15 ounce) can pinto beans with liquid, optional	425 g

- In a little oil, combine meats and onion in large roasting pan and brown. Add tomato sauce, tomatoes and green chilies, cumin, oregano, chili powder, 2 cups (480 ml) water and salt to taste. Bring to a boil, reduce heat and simmer for 2 hours.

- Add beans and heat until thoroughly hot.

Beefy Bean Chili

2 pounds lean ground beef	1 kg
3 ribs celery, sliced	
1 onion, chopped	
1 bell pepper, seeded, chopped	
2 teaspoons minced garlic	10 ml
1 (15 ounce) can tomato sauce	425 g
3 tablespoons chili powder	45 ml
2 (15 ounce) cans pinto beans with liquid	2 (425 g)
1 - 2 cups crushed tortilla chips	240 ml

- Brown and cook ground beef in large soup pot over medium heat until meat crumbles. Add celery, onion, bell pepper and minced garlic. Cook for 5 minutes or until vegetables are tender, but not brown.

- Stir in tomato sauce, chili powder, 2 cups (480 ml) water and salt and pepper to taste and mix well. Bring mixture to boil, reduce heat and simmer for 35 minutes.

- Add beans during last 15 minutes of cooking time. Ladle into individual serving bowls and top each serving with several tablespoons crushed tortilla chips.

Easy Chunky Chili

2 pounds premium-cut stew meat	1 kg
1 (10 ounce) can beef broth	280 g
1 onion, chopped	
2 (15 ounce) cans diced tomatoes	2 (425 g)
1 (10 ounce) can tomatoes and green chilies	280 g
2 (15 ounce) cans pinto beans with liquid	2 (425 g)
1 ½ tablespoons chili powder	22 ml
2 teaspoons ground cumin	10 ml
1 teaspoon ground oregano	5 ml

- If stew meat is in fairly large chunks, cut each chunk in half. Brown stew meat in large skillet and add all remaining ingredients.

- Boil, reduce heat and cook on low for at least 30 minutes.

If your soup is not intended as the main course, you can count on one quart to serve six people. As a main dish, plan on two servings per quart.

Baked Chili

1 ½ cups dried pinto beans	360 ml
1 ½ pounds beef round steak, cubed	360 ml
3 onions, finely chopped	
3 teaspoons minced garlic	15 ml
3 (8 ounce) cans tomato sauce	3 (227 g)
3 tablespoons chili powder	45 ml
1 tablespoon cumin	15 ml
½ teaspoon cayenne pepper	2 ml
Mexican-style 4-cheese blend	

- Preheat oven to 325° (162° C). Heat beans and 6 cups (1.5 L) water to boiling in Dutch oven and boil for 2 minutes.

- Stir in all remaining ingredients except cheese, cover and bake about 3 hours. Remove from oven and stir well. Return to oven to bake 1 more hour. Garnish each individual bowl with cheese.

Hearty Beef Chili

2 pounds round steak, cubed	1 kg
3 tablespoons oil, divided	45 ml
2 onions, chopped	
4 cloves garlic, minced	
¼ cup tomato paste	60 ml
2 - 4 canned jalapeno peppers, stemmed, seeded, minced	
3 tablespoons chili powder	45 ml
1 teaspoon oregano	5 ml
1 teaspoon cumin	5 ml
2 (15 ounce) cans diced tomatoes with liquid	2 (425 g)
1 (10 ounce) can beef broth	280 g
1 (7 ounce) can chopped green chilies	198 g
1 (15 ounce) can pinto beans, drained	425 g

- Heat 1 tablespoon (15 ml) oil in soup pot and brown beef. Transfer meat to bowl and set aside.

- Heat remaining 2 tablespoons (30 ml) oil in soup pot and add onion and garlic. Cook about 3 minutes, stir in tomato paste, jalapenos, chili powder, 1 teaspoon (5 ml) each of salt and pepper, oregano and cumin.

- Add tomatoes, meat, beef broth, 1 cup (240 ml) water and green chilies. Boil, reduce heat and simmer for 2 hours or until meat is tender and chili thickens. Stir in beans and continue simmering uncovered for about 20 minutes.

TIP: If you like it extra hot, leave the seeds and veins in the jalapenos. If you take the seeds out, rubber gloves will protect your hands from the juices.

Chile, New Mexico-Style

This New Mexico chile is also called "Chili Con Carne".

Vegetable oil
2 pounds chuck or pork roast, cubed   1 kg
2 (14 ounce) cans beef broth   2 (396 g)
6 - 8 dried New Mexico red chilies, ground
  or 4 - 5 dried chipotle chilies, ground
4 - 6 cloves garlic, minced
3 tablespoons paprika   45 ml
1 teaspoon cumin   5 ml
1 tablespoon oregano   15 ml

• Heat oil in large skillet or Dutch oven and brown meat on all sides. Add beef broth and ground chilies and bring to boil. Reduce heat, simmer about 2 hours and stir occasionally.

• Add garlic, paprika, cumin, oregano and 1 teaspoon (5 ml) salt. Cover and simmer for 15 minutes. Stir occasionally and skim grease.

Did you know that lettuce loves fat? Fat can be removed from hot soup by floating a large lettuce leaf on the surface.

Taco Chili

2 pounds very lean stew meat	1 kg
1 (14 ounce) can beef broth	396 g
2 (15 ounce) cans Mexican stewed tomatoes	2 (425 g)
1 (1 ounce) packet taco seasoning mix	28 g
2 (15 ounce) cans pinto beans with liquid	2 (425 g)
1 (15 ounce) can whole kernel corn with liquid	425 g
1 (8 ounce) package shredded Mexican 4-cheese blend	227 g

- Cut large pieces of stew meat in half and brown in large skillet.

- Combine stew meat, broth, tomatoes, taco seasoning mix, beans, corn and ¾ cup (180 ml) water in stew pot. (If you are not into "spicy", use original recipe stewed tomatoes instead of Mexican.)

- Boil, reduce heat and simmer for 1 hour or until meat is tender. Sprinkle in cheese on top when ready to serve.

    TIP: *For garnish top each serving with chopped green onions.*

Ancho-Spiked Chili

5 ancho chilies	
2 tablespoons oil	30 ml
2 onions, chopped	
2 cloves garlic, minced	
1 pound lean boneless beef, cubed	.5 kg
1 pound lean boneless pork, cubed	.5 kg
1 fresh or canned jalapeno pepper, seeded, minced	
1 teaspoon dried, crushed oregano	5 ml
1 teaspoon ground cumin	5 ml
½ cup dry red wine	120 ml

- Rinse ancho chilies, remove stems, seeds and veins and place in saucepan with 2 cups (480 ml) water. Boil, turn off heat and let stand, covered, for 30 minutes or until chilies soften. Pour chilies with liquid into blender and process until smooth.

- Heat oil in soup pot and saute onion, garlic and meats until meat is light brown. Add jalapeno pepper, 1 teaspoon (5 ml) salt, oregano, cumin, wine and ancho puree.

- Boil, reduce heat, cover and simmer for 2 hours. Uncover and simmer for about 30 minutes or until chili thickens slightly.

Chile Verde Con Carne

"Chile con carne" means chili with meat. Verde refers to the fresh green chilies.

2 - 3 pounds sirloin or tenderloin, cubed	1 kg
½ cup (1 stick) butter	120 ml
2 onions, chopped	
4 - 6 cloves garlic, minced	
8 - 10 fresh whole green chilies, peeled, seeded, chopped	
1 tablespoon ground cumin	15 ml
2 teaspoons oregano	10 ml

- Brown sirloin in butter in large skillet. Reduce heat to low and add all remaining ingredients plus 1 teaspoon (5 ml) each of salt and pepper. Simmer covered for about 2 to 3 hours.

- Stir occasionally and add ½ to 1 cup (120 ml) water if necessary. Remove cover, taste for flavor and adjust seasonings if needed.

TIP: To save time, chili powder may be used instead of roasting fresh green chilies, but the flavor of fresh chilies is the secret to the best chili.

Venison Chili

¼ pound salt pork, quartered	114 g
2 ½ pounds ground venison	1.2 kg
2 onions, chopped	
1 (15 ounce) can Mexican-style stewed	
tomatoes	425 g
¾ cup red wine	180 ml
2 teaspoons minced garlic	10 ml
3 tablespoons chili powder	45 ml
¾ teaspoon dried oregano	4 ml
1 teaspoon cumin	5 ml

- Brown salt pork in soup pot over medium heat. Add venison and onion, cook over medium to high heat until venison browns and crumbles and stir often.

- Stir in tomatoes, wine, garlic, chili powder, oregano, cumin, 1 cup (240 ml) water and salt to taste. Boil, reduce heat and simmer uncovered for 1 hour, stirring occasionally. Remove salt pork before serving.

Salty soup? If your sauce, soup or stew is too salty, add a peeled potato into the pot, and it will absorb the extra salt.

A Bowl of Red

Proper name for Real Texas Chili, make no beans about it.

At the 1st Original Terlingua International Cook-Off in Terlingua, Texas in 1966, Frunk Tolbert and Wick Fowler gave real Texas chili the name "Bowl of Red".

½ **cup beef suet or vegetable oil**	120 ml
3 **pounds sirloin steak, cubed**	1.3 kg
6 - 8 **dried chile colorado peppers, ground**	
or 4 - 5 dried chipotle chile peppers, ground	
1 - 2 **whole jalapeno peppers, divided**	
4 - 6 **cloves garlic, minced**	
½ **cup paprika**	120 ml
2 **tablespoons ground cumin**	30 ml
2 **tablespoons masa harina, optional**	30 ml

- Heat suet until fat separates from connective tissue or heat vegetable oil for healthier cooking. Remove suet and brown sirloin on all sides.

- Pour sirloin and oil from skillet in large pot or roasting pan. Add ground chile peppers, 1 whole jalapeno and enough water to be about 2 inches (5 cm) above meat.

- Bring water to boil, reduce heat and simmer about 2 to 3 hours. Stir occasionally and skim grease.

- Add garlic, paprika, cumin and 1 tablespoon (15 ml) salt, cover and simmer another 1 hour. Stir occasionally and skim grease.

- Check seasonings and if not hot enough, add whole jalapeno. Add masa harina if chili is too thin and simmer another 30 minutes to 1 hour.

TIP: Masa harina is flour made from masa, sun-dried or oven-dried corn kernels used to make corn tortillas.

Big-Time Chili

You know the chili's good when it makes your nose run.

2 onions, chopped	
¼ cup oil	60 ml
3 pounds lean ground beef	1.3 kg
1 (15 ounce) can diced tomatoes	425 g
1 (6 ounce) can tomato paste	168 g
¾ teaspoon cayenne pepper	4 ml
4 - 6 tablespoons chili powder	60 ml
2 teaspoons ground cumin	10 ml
1 tablespoon paprika	15 ml

- In roasting pan or pot, saute onions in oil and brown ground beef .

- Mix in all remaining ingredients with 2 teaspoons (10 ml) salt and bring to boil. Reduce heat and simmer for 3 hours.

- Stir several times and add water if needed.

Championship Chili

Real chili is worth the effort! Boy I mean!

Oil

3 - 3 ½ pounds stew meat	1.3 kg
1 onion chopped	
1 (15 ounce) can tomato sauce	425 g
10 - 12 tablespoons dried chile colorado peppers, ground, seeded	115 ml
1 - 2 tablespoons ground cumin	15 ml
1 tablespoon oregano	15 ml
1 - 2 jalapenos	

- In a little oil, brown stew meat and onion in large pot or roasting pan.

- Add tomato sauce, ground chilies, cumin, oregano, 1 tablespoon (15 ml) salt and enough water to be 2 inches (5 cm) above meat and bring to a boil. Reduce heat and simmer for about 2 hours. Stir occasionally.

- Taste for seasonings and add whole jalapeno if more "hot" is needed. Simmer another 1 hour.

- Serve immediately with crackers or wait until the next day to serve. Some people believe real chili needs time for flavors to blend.

TIP: Chiles Colorado are New Mexican Reds and are about 5 to7 inches (13 cm) long, about 1 to 2 (2.5 cm) inches wide, dark-red brown and slightly hot. If you have never ground dried chilies, use food processor, blender or coffee grinder. They will live through it and so will you. These are great peppers to use because you do not have to peel them when they are dry.

Perfect Pork Pleasers

Black Bean Soup

Half of the ingredients listed for this recipe are seasonings, so don't be scared about time and effort for this soup. It doesn't take much time to measure seasonings.

2 cups dried black beans	480 ml
1 cup diced ham	240 ml
1 onion, chopped	
1 carrot, chopped	
2 ribs celery, chopped	
3 jalapeno peppers, seeded, chopped	
2 (14 ounce) cans chicken broth	2 (396 g)
2 teaspoons cumin	10 ml
2 tablespoons snipped fresh cilantro	30 ml
1 teaspoon oregano	5 ml
1 teaspoon chili powder	5 ml
1 teaspoon cayenne pepper	5 ml
1 (8 ounce) carton sour cream	227 g

- Wash beans, soak overnight and drain. Except for sour cream, place all ingredients and 1 teaspoon (5 ml) salt with 10 cups (2 L) water in large, heavy soup pot. Boil, reduce heat and simmer for 3 hours or until beans are tender.

- Add more water as needed and stir occasionally. Make sure there is enough water in pot to make soup consistency and not too thick.

- Place few cups at a time in food processor (using steel blade) or blender and puree until smooth. Add sour cream and reheat soup. Serve in individual bowls.

Hearty Bean and Ham Soup

What a great supper for a cold winter night!

¼ cup (½ stick) butter	60 ml
1 (15 ounce) can sliced carrots, drained	415 g
1 cup chopped celery	240 ml
1 cup chopped green bell pepper	240 ml
2 - 3 cups cooked, diced ham	480 ml
2 (15 ounce) cans navy beans with liquid	2 (425 g)
2 (15 ounce) cans jalapeno pinto beans with liquid	2 (425 g)
2 (14 ounce) cans chicken broth	2 (396 g)
2 teaspoons chili powder	10 ml

- Cook carrots, celery and bell pepper in soup pot with butter about 8 minutes until tender-crisp.

- Add diced ham, navy beans, pinto beans, chicken broth, chili powder and salt and pepper to taste. Boil and stir constantly for 3 minutes. Reduce heat and simmer for 15 minutes.

TIP: Cornbread is great with this and it's so quick and easy to make. If you want to fix it, just buy 2 (8 ounce/227 g) packages corn muffin mix. Add 2 eggs and ⅔ cup (160 ml) milk, mix it up and pour it into greased 7 x 11-inch (18 x 28 cm) baking pan. Bake as package directs.

Pinto Bean Soup

2 (1 pound) packages dry pinto beans	2 (.5 kg)
1 smoked ham hock or 2 cups chopped ham	480 ml

- Wash beans, cover with cold water and soak overnight. Drain beans, cover with water and boil. Add ham, reduce heat and simmer slowly for 3 to 4 hours. (You may need to add more water.)

- When beans are tender, remove 2 to 3 cups (480 ml) beans and smash with potato masher. Return to pot and season with salt.

Frijole Soup

1 ½ pounds dried pinto beans	.7 kg
5 slices thick sliced bacon, cut in pieces	
2 onions, chopped	
1 teaspoon garlic powder	5 ml
½ teaspoon ground thyme	2 ml
½ teaspoon ground oregano	2 ml
½ teaspoon cayenne pepper	2 ml

- Wash beans, place in large soup pot and cover with water. Soak overnight and drain.

- Cook bacon and onions in skillet for about 5 minutes. Transfer with pan drippings to soup pot. Boil and add all seasonings. Lower heat and cook 4 hours. Add hot water when liquid goes below original level. When beans are done, remove about half of beans.

- Mash beans with potato masher or process in blender. Return to pot and add 1 tablespoon (15 ml) salt. Serve with hot, flour tortillas and butter.

Navy Bean Soup

This soup tastes great with cornbread.

3 (15 ounce) cans navy beans with liquid	3 (425 g)
1 (14 ounce) can chicken broth	396 g
1 cup chopped ham	240 ml
1 large onion, chopped	
½ teaspoon garlic powder	2 ml

- Combine all ingredients with 1 cup (240 ml) water in large saucepan and boil.

- Simmer until onion is tender-crisp and serve hot.

Good Ol' Bean Soup

3 tablespoons oil	45 ml
1 cup shredded carrots	240 ml
1 (16 ounce) package frozen, chopped onions and peppers	.5 kg
2 (14 ounce) cans chicken broth	2 (396 g)
2 (15 ounce) cans pinto beans with jalapenos with liquid	2 (425 g)
2 cups diced ham	480 ml

- Combine oil, carrots, onions and peppers in soup pot and cook for 10 minutes.

- Add broth, pinto beans, ham and ½ cup (120 ml) water. Boil, reduce heat and simmer for 15 minutes.

Ham Bone Soup

2 cups dried navy beans   480 ml
½ pound ham hock   227 g

- Cover beans in water and soak overnight.

- Drain and pour beans in large soup pot with 6 cups (1.5 L) water. Cook with ham hocks for 2 to 3 hours or until tender.

- Season with salt and pepper.

Tomato and White Bean Soup

2 tablespoons olive oil   30 ml
1 onion, chopped
1 green bell pepper, seeded, chopped
1 (15 ounce) can diced tomatoes   425 g
2 (14 ounce) cans chicken broth   2 (396 g)
2 (15 ounce) cans navy beans, rinsed, drained   2 (425 g)
1 ½ cups cubed ham   360 ml
½ cup chopped fresh parsley   120 ml

- Combine olive oil, onion, bell pepper in large saucepan and saute for 5 minutes and stir constantly.

- Stir in tomatoes, broth, navy beans and ham and bring to boil. Reduce heat and simmer for 10 minutes.

- Pour into individual soup bowls and sprinkle parsley on top.

Easy Cannellini Soup

4 strips bacon	
1 onion, chopped	
1 sweet red bell pepper, seeded, chopped	
2 teaspoons minced garlic	10 ml
3 (14 ounce) can chicken broth	3 (396 g)
1 (15 ounce) can cannellini beans, drained	425 g
1 teaspoon dried parsley	5 ml

- Fry bacon in soup pot, drain and save drippings in soup pot. Crumble bacon and set aside. Add onion, bell pepper and garlic to drippings and saute for 5 minutes, stirring occasionally. Stir in chicken broth, beans, ½ teaspoon (2 ml) pepper, parsley and salt to taste. Boil, reduce heat and simmer for 20 minutes. Sprinkle crumbled bacon over each serving of soup.

Soup With An Attitude

1 (32 ounce) carton chiken broth	1 kg
3 baked potatoes, peeled, grated	
2 onions, finely chopped	
3 ribs celery, sliced	
1 (8 ounce) can peas, drained	227 g
1 (7 ounce) can green chilies	198 g
3 cups chopped ham	710 ml
1 (16 ounce) package cubed Mexican	
processed cheese	.5 kg
1 (1 pint) half-and-half cream	.5 kg

- Combine broth, potatoes, onions, celery, peas, chilies and ham in soup pot. While stirring, bring to a boil, reduce heat to low-medium and simmer 30 minutes. On medium heat, add cheese and stir constantly until cheese melts. Stir in cream and continue cooking until soup is thoroughly hot; do no boil.

Bonzo Garbanzo Soup

1 (16 ounce) package frozen diced onions and bell peppers	.5 kg
1 pound Italian sausage, cut up	.5 kg
1 (14 ounce) can beef broth	396 g
1 (15 ounce) can Italian stewed tomatoes	425 g
2 (15 ounce) cans garbanzo beans, rinsed, drained	2 (425 g)

- Saute onions and bell peppers in soup pot with a little oil. Add Italian sausage and cook until brown. Stir in beef broth, stewed tomatoes and garbanzo beans.

- Boil mixture, reduce heat and simmer about 30 minutes.

Cabbage-Ham Soup

1 (16 ounce) package cabbage slaw	.5 kg
1 onion, chopped	
1 red bell pepper, seeded, chopped	
1 teaspoon minced garlic	5 ml
2 (14 ounce) cans chicken broth	2 (396 g)
1 (15 ounce) can stewed tomatoes	425 g
2 cups cooked, cubed ham	480 ml
¼ cup packed brown sugar	60 ml
2 tablespoons lemon juice	30 ml

- Combine cabbage, onion, bell pepper, garlic, chicken broth and 1 cup (240 ml) water in large, heavy soup pot. Boil, reduce heat and simmer for 20 minutes.

- Stir in tomatoes, ham, 1 teaspoon (5 ml) salt, brown sugar, lemon juice and pepper to taste. Heat just until soup is thoroughly hot.

Spicy Bean Soup

1 (15 ounce) can refried beans	425 g
1 (14 ounce) can chicken broth	396 g
2 (4 ounce) cans chopped green chilies	2 (114 g)
2 cloves garlic, minced	
2 - 3 jalapeno chilies, seeded, chopped	
1 teaspoon chili powder	5 ml
6 slices bacon	
1 bunch green onions with tops, chopped, divided	
5 ribs celery, chopped	
1 bell pepper, seeded, chopped	
1 (8 ounce) package shredded cheddar cheese	227 g

- Heat and whisk refried beans and chicken broth in large saucepan. Add green chilies, garlic, jalapenos, ¼ teaspoon (1 ml) pepper and chili powder and stir well. Reduce heat to low and stir occasionally.

- Fry bacon in skillet until crisp and saute about three-fourths onions, celery and bell pepper in pan drippings until onions are translucent.

- Crumble bacon and put into bean soup. Add onions, celery, bell peppers and pan drippings and stir well. Boil, reduce heat to low and serve immediately.

- Garnish with remaining onions and cheese.

Split Pea Soup

This is great for leftover ham.

1 (16 ounce) package dried green split peas	.5 kg
1 onion, chopped	
1 large potato, peeled, diced	
2 ribs celery, chopped	
1 cup shredded or chopped ham	240 ml
1 cup shredded carrots	240 ml
1 teaspoon minced garlic	5 ml
Croutons for garnish	

- Sort and rinse peas and place in large, heavy soup pot. Cover with water 2 inches (5 cm) above peas and soak overnight.

- Drain, add 2 quarts (2 L) water, onion, potato, celery, ham, carrots, garlic and salt and pepper to taste. Boil, reduce heat, cover and simmer for 2½ to 3 hours and stir occasionally. (If you happen to have a meaty ham bone, you can use that instead of chopped ham.)

- Cool slightly and process mixture in batches in blender until smooth. Return mixture to soup pot, cover and simmer for 5 minutes or until thoroughly hot. Garnish with seasoned croutons.

Lucky Pea Soup

Lucky Pea Soup is great on New Year's Day and they bring good luck in the New Year.

1 onion, chopped	
1 cup cooked, cubed ham	240 ml
1 (15 ounce) can black-eyed peas with	
jalapenos with liquid	425 g
1 (14 ounce) can chicken broth	396 g
1 teaspoon minced garlic	5 ml
1 teaspoon dried sage	5 ml

- Saute onion in a little oil in large saucepan. On high heat, add ham, black-eyed peas, broth, garlic and sage.

- Boil, reduce heat and simmer and stir occasionally for 20 minutes.

Split Pea and Tortellini Soup

⅓ cup dry split peas	80 ml
2 tablespoons dried minced onion	30 ml
1 ½ teaspoons dried basil	7 ml
1 tablespoon minced garlic	15 ml
½ cup shredded carrots	120 ml
1 (10 ounce) can tomatoes and green chilies	280 g
¾ cup cheese-filled tortellini	180 ml
1 cup cooked, diced ham	240 ml
2 (14 ounce) cans chicken broth	2 (396 g)

- Combine all ingredients with 1 ½ cups (360 ml) water in soup pot. Boil, reduce heat and simmer for 45 minutes or until peas are tender.

Old-Fashioned Hoppin' John

2 (15 ounce) cans black-eyed peas with	
jalapenos with liquid	2 (425 g)
1 (14 ounce) can chicken broth	396 g
1 teaspoon minced garlic	5 ml
½ cup uncooked, long-grain rice	120 ml
2 onions, finely chopped	
1 red bell pepper, seeded, chopped	
1 ½ cups cooked, cubed ham	360 ml
1 (8 ounce) package frozen mustard greens,	
coarsely chopped	227 g

- Combine peas, broth, 2 cups (480 ml) water, garlic, rice, onions and bell pepper in soup pot and boil. Reduce heat and simmer, stirring occasionally, until rice is tender, about 25 to 30 minutes. Stir in ham and greens and cook on medium heat for 5 to 10 minutes or until soup is thoroughly hot.

Soup That's Soul Food

3 (15 ounce) cans navy beans with liquid	3 (425 g)
2 onions, chopped	
2 teaspoons minced garlic	10 ml
3 potatoes, peeled, cubed	
2 cups diced ham	480 ml
2 (14 ounce) cans chicken broth	2 (396 g)
1 (10 ounce) package frozen chopped	
turnip greens	280 g

- Place 1 can beans in shallow bowl and mash with fork. Spray large soup pot and stir in mashed beans, remaining cans of beans, onions, garlic, potatoes, ham, broth, turnip greens, plus salt and pepper to taste. Bring to a boil and boil 5 minutes; reduce heat to low and simmer 45 minutes or until potatoes and greens are tender. Serve hot.

Rich Cheese Soup

5 slices bacon
1 small onion, finely chopped
2 ribs celery, finely sliced
1 medium leek, halved lengthwise, sliced
2 (14 ounce) cans chicken broth   2 (396 g)
⅔ cup quick-cooking oats
1 cup shredded Swiss cheese   240 ml
1 (8 ounce) carton whipping cream   227 g

- Cook bacon in large saucepan until crisp, drain and crumble. Save drippings in saucepan. Cook onion, celery and leek in pan drippings over medium heat for 10 minutes and stir often.

- Add broth and oats. Boil, reduce heat and simmer for 15 minutes. Cool slightly.

- Place half soup in blender and process until smooth. Repeat with remaining soup.

- Return all soup mixture to saucepan and stir in cheese and cream; heat until cheese melts. Do not boil. Ladle soup into bowl and sprinkle with crumbled bacon.

Tomato-Bacon Soup

1 (10 ounce) can tomato soup   280 g
1 (14 ounce) can stewed tomatoes with celery
  and peppers   396 g
3 slices bacon, fried, drained, crumbled

- Combine soup and stewed tomatoes. Heat thoroughly.

- Pour into soup bowls, sprinkle bacon on top and serve hot.

Creamed Broccoli Soup

4 slices bacon
1 small onion, minced
3 potatoes, shredded
1 (10 ounce) package frozen chopped broccoli   280 g
¼ cup (½ stick) butter   60 ml
3 tablespoons flour   45 ml
1 pint half-and-half cream   .5 kg

- Fry bacon in deep skillet, drain and set aside. With bacon
  drippings still in skillet, add onion, potatoes, 2 cups
  (480 ml) water and 1 teaspoon (5 ml) salt. Cover and cook
  about 10 minutes. Add broccoli and cook 5 minutes more.

- In separate large saucepan, melt butter and add flour. Stir
  and cook until mixture bubbles. Gradually add cream and
  cook and stir constantly until it thickens.

- Stir in potato-broccoli mixture and heat just until thoroughly
  hot. Crumble bacon and sprinkle on top of each serving.

Potato-Sausage Soup

1 pound pork sausage link	.5 kg
1 cup chopped celery	240 ml
1 cup chopped onion	240 ml
2 (10 ounce) cans potato soup	2 (280 g)
1 (14 ounce) can chicken broth	396 g

- Cut sausage into 1-inch (2.5 cm) diagonal slices. Brown sausage in large heavy soup pot, drain and place in separate bowl. Leave about 2 tablespoons (30 ml) sausage drippings in skillet and saute celery and onion.

- Add potato soup, ¾ cup (180 ml) water, chicken broth and sausage. Boil, reduce heat and simmer for 20 minutes.

Supper-Ready Potato Soup

1 (18 ounce) package frozen hash brown potatoes with onions and peppers, thawed	510 g
2 (14 ounce) cans chicken broth	2 (396 g)
3 ribs celery, finely chopped	
2 (10 ounce) cans cream of chicken soup	2 (280 g)
2 cups milk	480 ml
2 cups chopped ham	480 ml
2 teaspoons minced garlic	10 ml
1 teaspoon dried parsley flakes	5 ml

- Combine hash brown potatoes, broth and celery in large soup pot and boil. Reduce heat and simmer for 25 minutes.

- Pour in soup and milk and stir until mixture is smooth. Add ham, garlic, parsley and ½ teaspoon (2 ml) pepper. Boil, stir constantly, immediately reduce heat and simmer for 10 minutes.

Bacon-Potato Soup

2 (14 ounce) cans chicken broth seasoned
   with garlic   2 (396 g)
2 potatoes, peeled, cubed
1 onion, finely chopped
6 strips bacon, cooked, crumbled

- In large saucepan, combine broth, potatoes and onion in
  large saucepan. Bring to a boil, reduce heat to medium-
  high and boil about 10 minutes or until potatoes are tender.

- Season with a little pepper. Ladle into bowls and sprinkle
  with crumbled bacon.

Snap-Your-Fingers Potato Soup

2 (10 ounce) cans cream of potato soup   2 (280 g)
1 cup shredded cheddar cheese   240 ml
3 tablespoons real bacon bits   45 ml

- Heat potato soup with 1 cup (240 ml) water or milk in soup
  pot. Stir in cheese.

- Pour soup into soup bowls and sprinkle with bacon bits.

Green Chile Soup

5 slices bacon, cut into 1-inch pieces, divided	5 (2.5 cm)
1 onion, finely chopped	
2 ribs celery, finely chopped	
3 potatoes, peeled, cubed	
1 (7 ounce) can chopped green chilies	198 g
2 (14 ounce) cans chicken broth	2 (396 g)
1 pint half-and-half cream	.5 kg

- Fry bacon pieces until half done in soup pot. Put half bacon in separate bowl and set aside. Add onion and celery to soup pot and cook on medium heat until onion is translucent.

- Add potatoes, green chilies, chicken broth, ½ cup (120 ml) water and ½ teaspoon (2 ml) each of salt and pepper.

- Cook on low to medium heat until potatoes are tender, about 15 minutes. To make soup a little thicker, mash some potatoes with fork against sides of pan.

- When ready to serve, pour in cream and heat, but do not return to boil. Microwave remaining bacon until crisp. Sprinkle bacon on top of each serving to garnish.

Do you live in an altitude higher than 2,500 feet? If so, you may need to extend the cooking time since liquids boil at a lower temperature.

Cowboy Sausage-Bean Soup

1 pound pork sausage	.5 kg
2 (15 ounce) cans pinto beans	2 (425 g)
2 (15 ounce) cans stewed tomatoes	2 (425 g)
1 onion, chopped	
¼ teaspoon garlic powder	1 ml
½ teaspoon thyme	2 ml
1 tablespoon chili powder	15 ml
¼ teaspoon dried coriander	1 ml
1 large potato, peeled, diced	
1 bell pepper, chopped	
1 (8 ounce) package cubed processed cheese	227 g
½ cup grated Monterey Jack cheese	120 ml

- Brown sausage in large, heavy soup pot and drain fat. Add beans, tomatoes, 1 quart (1 L) water, onions, 1 teaspoon (5 ml) salt, garlic powder, thyme, chili powder, coriander and ¼ teaspoon (1 ml) pepper.

- Boil, reduce heat and cover. Simmer for 1 hour. Add potatoes and bell pepper, cover and simmer another 30 minutes or until potatoes are soft, but not mushy.

- Stir in processed cheese and heat just until it melts. To serve, sprinkle each serving with Monterey Jack cheese.

Sausage-Tortellini Soup

1 pound Italian sausage	.5 kg
1 onion, chopped	
3 ribs celery, sliced	
2 (14 ounce) cans beef broth	2 (396 g)
½ teaspoon dried basil	2 ml
1 (15 ounce) can sliced carrots, drained	425 g
1 medium zucchini, halved, sliced	
1 (10 ounce) can Italian stewed tomatoes	280 g
1 (9 ounce) package refrigerated	
meat-filled tortellini	255 g
Mozzarella cheese	

- Cook and stir sausage, onion and celery on medium heat in soup pot until sausage is light brown.

- Drain and stir in beef broth, 1½ cups (360 ml) water, basil, carrots, zucchini, tomatoes, tortellini and salt and pepper to taste.

- Boil, reduce heat and simmer for 20 minutes or until tortellini are tender.

- Ladle into individual soup bowls and sprinkle each serving with cheese.

Supper-Sausage Soup

1 pound bulk Italian sausage	.5 kg
1 (16 ounce) package frozen onions and peppers	.5 kg
2 (14 ounce) cans stewed tomatoes	2 (396 g)
1 (4 ounce) can sliced mushrooms, drained	114 g
2 (14 ounce) cans beef broth	2 (396 g)
¾ cup hot salsa	180 ml
1 teaspoon dried basil	5 ml
1 teaspoon sugar	5 ml
Shredded mozzarella cheese	

- Brown and cook sausage, onions and peppers in soup pot until sausage crumbles.

- Stir in tomatoes, mushrooms, broth, salsa, basil, sugar and salt and pepper to taste. Boil, reduce heat and simmer for about 15 minutes.

- Before serving, sprinkle a little cheese over each serving.

Sausage-Vegetable Soup

1 pound bulk Italian sausage	.5 kg
2 onions, chopped	
2 teaspoons minced garlic	10 ml
1 (1 ounce) packet beefy soup mix	28 g
1 (15 ounce) can sliced carrots, drained	425 g
2 (15 ounce) cans Italian stewed tomatoes	2 (425 g)
2 (15 ounce) cans garbanzo beans, drained	2 (425 g)
1 cup uncooked elbow macaroni	240 ml

- Brown sausage, onions and garlic in large soup pot. Drain and add 4 cups (1 L) water, soup mix, carrots, tomatoes and garbanzo beans. Boil, reduce heat and simmer for 25 minutes. Add elbow macaroni and continue cooking another 15 to 20 minutes or until macaroni is tender.

Wild Rice and Ham Soup

1 (6 ounce) box long-grain wild rice	168 g
1 (16 ounce) package frozen onions and bell peppers	.5 kg
1 (10 ounce) can cream of celery soup	280 g
2 (14 ounce) cans chicken broth	2 (396 g)
2 cups diced ham	480 ml
2 (15 ounce) cans black-eyed peas with jalapenos with liquid	2 (425 g)
1 (8 ounce) carton sour cream	227 g

- Cook rice according to package directions.

- In soup pot, combine rice, onions and bell peppers, celery soup, broth, ham and black-eyed peas. Bring to a boil, reduce heat and simmer for 20 minutes.

- When ready to serve, stir in sour cream.

Some of the greatest artists in history were inspired by soup: Pablo Picasso painted "La Soup;" Vincent Van Gosh painted "Bowls and Bottles;" and James McNeill Whistler painted "Soupe a Trois Sous."

Easy Pork Tenderloin Stew

Cornbread or hot biscuits are really good with this stew.

2 - 3 cups cubed, cooked pork	480 ml
1 (12 ounce) jar pork gravy	340 g
¼ cup chili sauce	60 ml
1 (16 ounce) package frozen stew vegetables	.5 kg

- Combine cubed pork, gravy, chili sauce, stew vegetables and ½ cup (120 ml) water in stew pot. Boil for 2 minutes, reduce heat and simmer for 10 minutes.

Southern Gumbo

This is great for leftover ham and no one will know it's a "leftover" meal.

2 tablespoons butter	30 ml
2 tablespoons flour	30 ml
1 (14 ounce) can chicken broth	396 g
1 (15 ounce) can diced tomatoes	425 g
1 cup shredded ham	240 ml
2 cups fresh, sliced okra	480 ml

- Mix butter and flour in large saucepan. Cook over medium heat and stir constantly until a paste-like roux turns light brown. Stir in broth, tomatoes, ham and okra and bring to boil.

- Reduce heat to low and simmer for 25 minutes, stirring often, until gumbo thickens slightly.

Pancho Villa Stew

1 pound smoked sausage	.5 kg
3 cups diced, cooked ham	710 ml
3 (14 ounce) cans chicken broth	3 (396 g)
1 (15 ounce) can diced tomatoes with liquid	425 g
2 (7 ounce) cans chopped green chilies	2 (198 g)
1 large onion, chopped	
1 teaspoon garlic powder	5 ml
2 teaspoons ground cumin	10 ml
2 teaspoons cocoa	10 ml
1 teaspoon dried oregano	5 ml
2 (15 ounce) cans pinto beans with liquid	2 (425 g)
1 (15 ounce) can hominy with liquid	425 g
1 (8 ounce) can whole kernel corn, drained	227 g

- Cut sausage into ½-inch (1.2 cm) slices. Combine ham, sausage, broth, tomatoes, green chilies, onion, garlic powder, cumin, cocoa, oregano and ½ teaspoon (2 ml) salt in roasting pan. Boil, reduce heat and simmer for 45 minutes.

- Add pinto beans, hominy and corn and boil. Reduce heat and simmer another 15 minutes.

- Serve with buttered, flour tortillas or cornbread.

A pinch of red pepper flakes makes a wonderful addition to most soups.

Hearty Ranch-Bean Stew

½ pound lean beef stew meat	227 g
1 pound pork loin, cubed	.5 kg
2 tablespoons oil	30 ml
1 (14 ounce) can beef broth	396 g
2 (15 ounce) cans ranch-style beans with liquid	2 (425 g)
2 (15 ounce) cans Mexican stewed tomatoes	2 (425 g)
1 (11 ounce) can mexicorn	312 g
1 green bell pepper, chopped	
1 (1 ounce) packet ranch dressing mix	28 g
1 teaspoon ground cumin	5 ml
1 ancho chile	
Crushed tortilla chips	

- Brown beef and pork meats in hot oil in heavy stew pot and season with salt and pepper to taste. Add beef broth and heat to boiling. Reduce heat and simmer for 30 minutes.

- Add beans, tomatoes, corn, bell pepper, dressing mix, cumin, ancho chile and ½ cup (120 ml) water; simmer for about 20 minutes.

- Before serving, remove ancho chile. Serve in bowl with handful of crushed chips on top of each serving.

  TIP: If you don't want to use an ancho chile, just add chili powder to taste.

  Ancho chiles are dried poblano chilies that are about 3 to 4 inches long and turn from bright green to dark red when dried. They are mild and a little on the sweet side as far as chilies go.

Pecos Pork Stew

2 pounds boneless pork shoulder, cubed	1 kg
1 (16 ounce) package frozen chopped onions and peppers	.5 kg
2 cloves garlic, minced	
¼ cup fresh chopped cilantro	60 ml
3 tablespoons chili powder	45 ml
2 (14 ounce) cans chicken broth	2 (396 g)
2 cups peeled, cubed potatoes	480 ml
1 (16 ounce) package frozen corn	.5 kg

- Brown meat in a little oil in large roaster. Stir in onions, bell peppers, garlic, cilantro, chili powder, 1 teaspoon (5 ml) salt and chicken broth.

- Cover and cook on medium heat for about 45 minutes or until pork is tender.

- Add potatoes and corn. Boil, turn heat down to medium and cook another 30 minutes. Serve with cornbread.

Southwest Pork Stew

2 tablespoons oil	3 ml
2 onions, chopped	
1 green bell pepper, seeded, chopped	
3 teaspoons minced garlic	15 ml
2 pounds pork tenderloin, cubed	1 kg
2 (14 ounce) cans chicken broth	2 (396 g)
2 baking potatoes, peeled, cubed	
2 (15 ounce) cans Mexican stewed tomatoes	2 (425 g)
1 (15 ounce) can yellow hominy, drained	425 g
2 teaspoons chili powder	10 ml
1 teaspoon ground cumin	5 ml
1 tablespoon lime juice	5 ml

- Place oil in stew pot and saute onion, bell pepper and garlic for 5 minutes.

- Add cubed pork and chicken broth and boil. Reduce heat and simmer for 25 minutes.

- Add potatoes and cook another 15 minutes or until potatoes are tender. Stir in tomatoes, hominy, chili powder, cumin, lime juice and salt to taste. Heat just until stew is thoroughly hot.

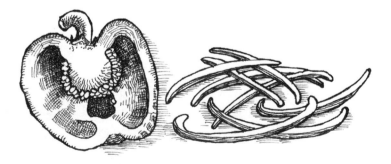

Polish-Vegetable Stew

1 onion, sliced	
2 carrots, sliced	
1 bell pepper, seeded, chopped	
2 (15 ounce) cans stewed tomatoes	2 (425 g)
2 (15 ounce) cans new potatoes, drained, quartered	2 (425 g)
1 pound Polish sausage, sliced	.5 kg
1 (9 ounce) package fresh coleslaw mix	255 g

- Place a little oil in large stew pot. Cook onion, carrot slices and bell peppers for 3 minutes or until tender-crisp. Add tomatoes and stir well. Stir potatoes and sausage in soup mixture. Boil, reduce heat and simmer for 10 minutes. Stir in coleslaw mix and cook on medium heat for another 8 minutes, stirring occasionally.

Black Bean Stew Supper

1 pound pork sausage link, thinly sliced	.5 kg
2 onions, chopped	
3 ribs celery, sliced	
3 (15 ounce) cans black beans, drained, rinsed	3 (425 g)
2 (10 ounce) cans diced tomatoes and green chilies	2 (280 g)
2 (14 ounce) cans chicken broth	2 (396 g)

- Place sausage slices, onion and celery in stew pot with a little oil, cook until sausage is light brown and onion is soft and drain. Add beans, tomatoes and green chilies and broth. Boil, reduce heat and simmer for 30 minutes. Take out about 2 cups (480 ml) stew mixture, pour into food processor and pulse until almost smooth. Return mixture to pot and stir to thicken stew. Return heat to high until stew is thoroughly hot.

Ham and Sausage Stew

3 cups cooked, diced ham	710 ml
1 pound Polish sausage, sliced	.5 kg
3 (14 ounce) cans chicken broth	3 (396 g)
2 (15 ounce) cans Mexican stewed tomatoes	2 (425 g)
1 tablespoon ground cumin	15 ml
2 (15 ounce) cans navy beans with liquid	2 (425 g)
2 (15 ounce) cans whole kernel corn, drained	2 (425 g)

- Combine ham, sausage, chicken broth, tomatoes, cumin and salt to taste in large roaster.

- Add a little oil and cook on high heat for about 5 minutes.

- Add navy beans and corn, reduce heat and simmer for 35 minutes. Serve with warmed, buttered flour tortillas.

Turnip Greens Stew

2 cups chopped cooked ham	480 ml
2 (14 ounce) cans chicken broth	2 (396 g)
2 (16 ounce) packages frozen chopped turnip greens	2 (.5 kg)
1 (16 ounce) package frozen, chopped onions and bell peppers	.5 kg
1 (10 ounce) package frozen corn	280 g
1 teaspoon sugar	5 ml

- Combine all ingredients with 1 teaspoon (5 ml) pepper in large stew pot. Boil, cover, reduce heat and simmer, stirring occasionally for 25 minutes.

Ham and Lentil Stew

1 (1 ounce) packet onion-mushroom soup mix	28 g
1 (14 ounce) can chicken broth	396 g
1 cup lentils, rinsed, drained	240 ml
1 cup uncooked brown rice	240 ml
2 cups chopped onion	480 ml
2 cups chopped celery	480 ml
2 (15 ounce) cans diced tomatoes with liquid	2 (425 g)
1 (15 ounce) can sliced carrots, drained	425 g
2 cups cooked, cubed ham	480 ml
1 tablespoon apple-cider vinegar	15 ml

- Combine soup mix, chicken broth, lentils, rice, onions, celery and 2 cups (480 ml) water in stew pot. Boil, reduce heat and simmer for 45 minutes.

- On medium heat, stir in tomatoes, carrots, ham and vinegar and cook until mixture is thoroughly hot.

Southern Turnip Greens Stew

2 (16 ounce) packages frozen chopped turnip greens	2 (.5 kg)
1 (10 ounce) package frozen diced onions and bell peppers	280 g
2 cups chopped, cooked ham	480 ml
2 (15 ounce) cans chicken broth	2 (425 g)

- Combine turnip greens, onions, bell peppers, ham, chicken broth and 1 teaspoon (5 ml) pepper in stew pot.

- Boil, reduce heat, cover and simmer for 30 minutes.

Ham and Fresh Okra Soup

1 ham hock	
1 cup frozen butter beans or lima beans	240 ml
1½ pounds chicken or ham, cooked, cubed	.7 kg
1 (15 ounce) can stewed tomatoes	425 g
3 cups small, whole okra	710 ml
2 large onions, diced	
Cooked Rice	

- Boil ham hock in 1½ quarts (1.5 L) water for about 1 hour 30 minutes in soup pot. Add remaining ingredients with salt and pepper to taste and simmer 1 more hour. Remove ham hock and serve over hot, cooked rice.

Posole

Posole is a traditional dish made famous in Jalisco, Mexico. Families pass recipes through generations and all have opinions about the ingredients for their special dish. This recipe is a faster version than the typical all-day soups or stews.

1 pound pork boneless shoulder, cubed	.5 kg
¼ cup flour	60 ml
¼ cup oil	60 ml
1 clove garlic, minced	
1 onion, chopped	
1 (15 ounce) can pinto beans with liquid	425 g
1 (7 ounce) can chopped green chilies	198 g
1 - 2 teaspoons fresh, chopped cilantro	5 ml
½ teaspoon cayenne pepper	2 ml
2 (14 ounce) cans chicken broth	2 (396 g)
1 (15 ounce) can hominy, drained	425 g
1 ½ teaspoons dried oregano leaves	7 ml

- Dredge pork in flour and brown in oil in soup pot. Add garlic and onion, saute until onion is translucent and drain excess oil.

- Stir in beans, green chilies, cilantro, cayenne pepper and chicken broth. Boil and simmer, covered, for about 45 minutes.

- Stir in hominy, 1 teaspoon (5 ml) salt and oregano leaves and simmer 15 to 20 minutes.

Quick-Step Posole

1 ½ - 2 pounds boneless pork shoulder, cubed	.7 kg
¼ cup flour	60 ml
2 tablespoons oil	30 ml
2 onions, chopped	
1 clove garlic, minced	
2 ribs celery, chopped	
1 (8 ounce) can hominy, drained	227 g
1 (10 ounce) bottle red chili sauce	280 g

- Season pork with 1 teaspoon (5 ml) salt and ½ teaspoon (2 ml) pepper and dredge in flour on all sides.

- Heat oil in large saucepan and brown pork. Add onions, garlic and celery; cook until onions are translucent.

- Add hominy and red chili sauce to saucepan and cook on low, covered, until pork is tender. Stir occasionally.

Ham and Corn Chowder

3 medium potatoes, cubed	
2 (14 ounce) cans chicken broth, divided	2 (396 g)
2 ribs celery, chopped	
1 onion, chopped	
4 tablespoons flour	60 ml
1 pint half-and-half cream	.5 kg
½ teaspoon cayenne pepper	.5 ml
1 (15 ounce) can whole kernel corn	425 g
1 (15 ounce) can cream-style corn	425 g
3 cups cooked, cubed ham	710 ml
1 (8 ounce) package shredded processed cheese	227 g

- Cook potatoes with 1 can chicken broth in saucepan. Saute celery and onion in large soup pot with a little oil.

- On medium heat add flour and mix well. Add second can broth and half-and-half. Cook, stirring constantly, until mixture thickens.

- Add potatoes, cayenne pepper, corn, cream-style corn, ham, cheese and salt and pepper to taste. Heat slowly and stir several times to keep from sticking.

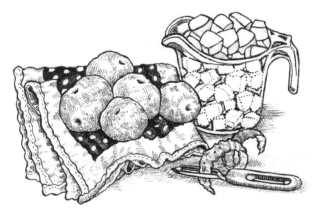

Ham Chowder

This is a real tasty way to use leftover ham. It has a great flavor!

1 cup sliced celery	240 ml
½ cup chopped onion	120 ml
2 tablespoons (¼ stick) butter	30 ml
3 cups shredded cabbage	710 ml
3½ cups cooked diced ham	830 ml
2 (15 ounce) cans Mexican-style stewed tomatoes with liquid	2 (425 kg)
1 (15 ounce) can whole kernel corn, drained	425 g
1 (15 ounce) can whole potatoes, drained, sliced	425 g
1 (14 ounce) can chicken broth	396 g
½ cup ketchup	120 ml
¼ cup packed light brown sugar	60 ml
½ teaspoon garlic powder	2 ml

- Saute celery and onion in butter in large roasting pan or soup pot over medium heat.

- Add remaining ingredients plus 1 cup (240 ml) water and ½ teaspoon (2 ml) salt and bring to boil. Reduce heat, cover and simmer for 1 hour.

Veggie-Ham Chowder

1 large onion, chopped	
3 ribs celery, sliced	
3 cups shredded cabbage	710 ml
3 cups cooked, cubed ham	710 ml
2 (15 ounce) cans stewed tomatoes	2 (425 g)
1 (15 ounce) can whole kernel corn, drained	425 g
1 (15 ounce) can whole new potatoes, sliced	425 g
2 (14 ounce) cans chicken broth	2 (396 g)
1 cup thick and chunky salsa	240 ml

- Saute onion and celery in large soup pot with a little oil over medium to high heat. Add remaining ingredients, boil, reduce heat and simmer for 30 minutes.

Easy Veggie-Ham Chowder

1 carrot, grated	
2 ribs celery, sliced	
1 onion, chopped	
1 (4.5 ounce) box julienne potato mix	128 g
3 cups milk	710 ml
2 cups cooked, cubed ham	480 ml
Sharp cheddar cheese	

- Combine 2 ¾ cups (660 ml) water with carrot, celery, onion and potato mix in soup pot. Boil, reduce heat, cover and simmer for 20 minutes.

- Stir in milk and packet of sauce mix from potatoes, mix well and boil. Simmer for 2 minutes and stir in ham. Before serving, garnish with sharp cheddar cheese.

Caraway-Potato Chowder

1 (18 ounce) package frozen hash brown potatoes	510 g
1 onion, chopped	
1 red bell pepper, seeded, chopped	
1 (14 ounce) can chicken broth	396 g
1 (10 ounce) can cream of celery soup	280 g
1 pint half-and-half cream	.5 kg
2 teaspoons caraway seeds, crushed	10 ml
1 ½ cups cooked, chopped ham	360 ml
½ teaspoon seasoned lemon pepper	2 ml

- Combine hash browns, onion, bell pepper and chicken broth in large saucepan.

- Boil, reduce heat and simmer for 10 to 15 minutes or until potatoes are tender. Do not drain.

- On medium heat, stir constantly and add celery soup, cream, caraway seeds, ham and lemon pepper. Heat just until thoroughly hot.

To make a good base for your soup, you can use any of the following: canned soups, such as cream of mushroom soup, canned tomatoes, tomato juice, canned chicken broth, homemade stocks, commercial soup bases, clam or seafood broth and the addition of some bacon.

Potato-Ham Chowder

This is a great recipe to use when you have leftover ham!

3 medium potatoes	
2 (14 ounce) cans chicken broth, divided	2 (396 g)
5 tablespoons butter	75 ml
2 ribs celery, chopped	
1 onion, chopped	
2 (10 ounce) cans nacho cheese soup	2 (280 g)
1 (16 ounce) package frozen corn	.5 kg
1 (15 ounce) can cream-style corn	425 g
1 (1 pint) carton half-and-half cream	.5 kg
3 cups cubed ham	710 ml

- Peel potatoes, cut in small chunks and cook with 1 can chicken broth.

- Melt butter and saute celery and onion in large soup pot. Add cheese soup and remaining can of chicken broth, stir constantly and cook until slightly thick.

- Add cooked potatoes with liquid and remaining ingredients plus 1½ teaspoons (7 ml) salt and ½ teaspoon (2 ml) pepper. Heat slowly and stir several times to keep from sticking.

   TIP: This will only serve 6 to 8 because everyone will want a second bowl.

Rich Corn Chowder

8 ears fresh corn	
8 slices bacon	
1 small onion, chopped	
½ red bell pepper, seeded, chopped	
1 small baking potato, peeled, cubed	
1 pint half-and-half cream	.5 kg
2 teaspoons sugar	10 ml
½ teaspoon dried thyme	2 ml
1 tablespoon cornstarch	15 ml

- Cut corn from cobs into large bowl and scrape well to remove all milk.

- Fry bacon in large soup pot over medium heat, remove bacon and save drippings in pan. Crumble bacon and set aside.

- Cook onion and bell pepper in drippings until tender. Stir in corn, potato, 1 cup (240 ml) water and salt and pepper to taste. Boil, cover, reduce heat and simmer for 15 minutes, stirring occasionally.

- Stir in 1½ cups (360 ml) cream, sugar and thyme. Combine cornstarch and remaining cream and stir until smooth. Gradually add to corn mixture and stir constantly.

- Cook uncovered for 15 minutes, stirring constantly, until soup thickens.

Sausage Chowder

1 pound pork sausage	.5 kg
2 (15 ounce) cans kidney beans, rinsed, drained	2 (425 g)
1 (15 ounce) can diced tomatoes	425 g
1 medium potato, peeled, cubed	
1 green bell pepper, seeded, chopped	
1 onion, chopped	
1 teaspoon minced garlic	5 ml
¼ teaspoon thyme	1 ml

- Brown and cook sausage in large soup pot and drain. Add beans, tomatoes, potatoes, bell pepper, onion, garlic, thyme and salt and pepper to taste. Boil, reduce heat and simmer for 1 hour.

Sausage-Bean Chowder

2 pounds pork sausage	1 kg
1 (15 ounce) can pinto beans with liquid	425 g
1 (15 ounce) can navy beans with liquid	425 g
1 (15 ounce) can kidney beans, drained	425 g
2 (15 ounce) cans Mexican stewed tomatoes	2 (425 g)
2 (14 ounce) cans chicken broth	2 (396 g)
1 teaspoon minced garlic	5 ml

- Brown and cook sausage in soup pot and stir until sausage crumbles. Add 3 cans beans, tomatoes, broth and garlic and boil. Reduce heat to low and simmer for 20 minutes.

Sausage and Corn Chowder

⅓ pound hot Italian sausage	150 g
2 (11 ounce) cans mexicorn with liquid	2 (312 g)
3 (14 ounce) cans chicken broth	3 (396 g)

- Remove casing from sausage, place in skillet, crumble and cook over medium heat. Stir in corn and chicken broth. Mix well and simmer for 10 minutes or until hot.

Green Chile-Corn Chowder

¼ pound bacon	114 g
1 medium onion, minced	
1 (15 ounce) can whole kernel corn with liquid	425 g
1 (15 ounce) can Mexican-style stewed tomatoes	425 g
2 - 3 fresh green chilies, roasted, peeled, seeded, chopped	
2 large baking potatoes, peeled, cubed	
1 teaspoon sugar	5 ml
1 teaspoon paprika	5 ml
1 (5 ounce) can evaporated milk	143 g

- Cut bacon into very small pieces and fry to crisp in skillet. Add onion and cook until translucent. Transfer to soup pot.

- Add corn with liquid, tomatoes, chilies, potatoes, sugar, ½ teaspoon (2 ml) salt, ¼ teaspoon (1 ml) pepper, paprika and 3 cups (710 ml) boiling water.

- Cook on low to medium until potatoes are tender. Remove from heat and slowly stir in evaporated milk. Serve immediately.

Satisfying Seafood Delights

Spiked-Crab Soup

1 (1 ounce) packet dry onion soup mix	28 g
1 (6 ounce) can crabmeat with liquid, flaked	168 g
1 (8 ounce) carton whipping cream	227 g
½ cup white wine	120 ml

- Dissolve soup mix with 2 cups (480 ml) water in saucepan. Add crabmeat, crab liquid and whipping cream. Season with a little salt and pepper.

- Heat, but do not boil and simmer for 20 minutes. Stir in wine, heat and serve warm.

Carolina She-Crab Soup

4 cups milk	1 L
¼ teaspoon mace	1 ml
1 teaspoon lemon zest	5 ml
1 pound crabmeat, flaked	.5 kg
1 (1 pint) carton whipping cream	.5 kg
¼ cup (½ stick) butter	60 ml
½ cup cracker crumbs, divided	120 ml
2 tablespoons sherry	30 ml

- Pour milk, mace and lemon zest in double boiler and simmer for 5 minutes. Add crabmeat, cream and butter and cook over low heat for 15 minutes.

- Stir in cracker crumbs a little at a time to get consistency desired and season soup with salt and pepper.

- Cover, remove from heat and set aside for 5 to 10 minutes so flavors blend. Add sherry before serving.

Oyster Soup

2 (14 ounce) cans chicken broth	2 (396 g)
1 large onion, chopped	
3 ribs celery, sliced	
1 red bell pepper, seeded, chopped	
2 teaspoons minced garlic	10 ml
2 pints fresh oysters, rinsed, drained	1 kg
½ cup (1 stick) butter	120 ml
¼ cup flour	60 ml
2 cups milk	480 ml
1 tablespoon dried parsley	15 ml

- Combine broth, onion, celery, bell pepper and garlic in soup pot. Boil, reduce heat and simmer, stirring occasionally, for 30 minutes.

- Boil oysters in 2 cups (480 ml) water in saucepan for 2 minutes, stirring often, or until edges of oysters begin to curl.

- Remove oysters, coarsely chop half and set aside. Pour oyster stock into soup pot with vegetables.

- Melt butter in saucepan over medium heat, gradually whisk in flour and cook for 1 minute. Add flour mixture to soup pot and simmer, stirring occasionally, over medium heat for 3 minutes.

- Stir in chopped oysters, milk, parsley and salt and pepper to taste. Cook and stir occasionally over medium heat for 8 minutes or until mixture thickens. Stir in remaining whole oysters.

Crab Bisque

1 (10 ounce) can cream of celery soup	280 g
1 (10 ounce) can pepper-pot soup	280 g
1 pint half-and-half cream	.5 kg
1 (6 ounce) can crabmeat, drained, flaked	168 g
Scant ⅓ cup sherry	80 ml

- Mix soups and cream. Stir in crabmeat and heat through.

- Just before serving, add sherry and stir.

Seafood Bisque

¼ cup (½ stick) butter	60 ml
1 (8 ounce) package frozen salad shrimp, thawed	227 g
1 (6 ounce) can crab, drained, flaked	168 g
1 (15 ounce) can whole new potatoes, drained, sliced	425 g
1 teaspoon minced garlic	5 ml
½ cup flour	120 ml
2 (14 ounce) cans chicken broth, divided	2 (396 g)
1 cup half-and-half cream	240 ml

- Melt butter and cook on medium heat in large saucepan. Add shrimp, crab, new potatoes and garlic and cook for 10 minutes.

- Stir in flour and cook, stirring constantly, for 3 minutes. Gradually add chicken broth, cook and stir until mixture thickens.

- Stir in cream and salt and pepper to taste, stirring constantly, and cook just until mixture is thoroughly hot; do not boil.

Easy Oyster Stew

3 fresh green onions, finely chopped	
2 tablespoons butter	30 ml
1 (12 ounce) container oysters with liquor	340 g
1 pint whipping cream	.5 kg
2 cups milk	480 ml

- Saute green onions in butter in stew pot. Add oysters, cream, milk, cayenne pepper and salt and pepper to taste.

- Cook over low heat until oyster edges begin to curl and mixture is hot, but not boiling.

Creole Soup

2 tablespoons butter	30 ml
1 (16 ounce) package frozen chopped onions and peppers	.5 kg
2 ribs celery, sliced	
1 teaspoon minced garlic	5 ml
1 (6 ounce) package garlic, butter-flavored rice	168 g
2 (15 ounce) cans stewed tomatoes	2 (425 g)
1 teaspoon Creole seasoning	5 ml
1 (8 ounce) package frozen salad shrimp, thawed	227 g

- Melt butter and saute onions, peppers, celery and garlic in large skillet. Stir in 1 cup (240 ml) water, rice, tomatoes and Creole seasoning and boil.

- Reduce heat to medium and cook, stirring often, for 6 minutes. Add shrimp, cover and simmer for 5 more minutes.

    TIP: If you want a little snap to this stew, add cayenne pepper to taste.

Low Country Crab Soup

1 onion, quartered	
1 medium leek, white only	
1 carrot, scraped, cut into 1-inch pieces	2.5 cm
3 ribs celery, cut into 1-inch pieces	2.5 cm
¼ cup (½ stick) butter, divided	60 ml
1 teaspoon minced garlic	5 ml
¼ cup flour	60 ml
1 (14 ounce) can chicken broth	396 g
2 (1 pint) cartons half-and-half cream, divided	2 (.5 kg)
1 tablespoon seafood seasoning	15 ml
¼ teaspoon cayenne pepper	1 ml
1 pound fresh lump crabmeat, flaked, drained	.5 kg
¼ cup brandy	60 ml
1 tablespoon chopped fresh parsley	15 ml

- Puree onion, leek, carrot and celery in blender. Melt 2 tablespoons (30 ml) butter in soup pot over medium heat, add pureed vegetables and garlic. Cook for 8 minutes, covered and stir often.

- Stir in flour, cook 1 minute and stir often. Gradually stir in broth, 1 pint (.5 kg) cream, seasoning, cayenne pepper and salt and pepper to taste. Cook for 10 minutes and stir occasionally.

- In small skillet, melt remaining butter, add crabmeat, toss gently over medium heat until thoroughly hot; stir in brandy.

- Stir crabmeat mixture, parsley and remaining cream into vegetables in soup pot. Heat until thoroughly hot.

Frogmore Stew

Frogmore Stew originated in South Carolina's Low Country and dates back many years. According to one story passed down through the years, an old fisherman gathered up whatever he could find to put in a stew. Other stories credit specific people on St. Helena Island with the invention, but there's no disagreement to the fact that Frogmore Stew is a combination of sausage, seafood and corn. Here's one version of the famous dish.

3 tablespoons seafood seasoning	45 ml
3 pounds smoked link sausage, sliced	1.3 kg
3 onions, peeled, chopped	
1 lemon, sliced, seeded	
½ cup (1 stick) butter	120 ml
6 ears corn, halved	
3 pounds large shrimp, peeled	1.3 kg

- Combine about 2 gallons (8 L) water, seasoning, sausage, onions, lemon, salt and pepper to taste in very large stew pot and boil. Simmer uncovered for 45 minutes.

- Add butter and corn and cook for 10 minutes. Add shrimp, cook for 5 more minutes and drain water. Serve immediately.

When reheating soup, use a double boiler. The hot water in the bottom part of the boiler does the trick with no burned or boiled-over soup.

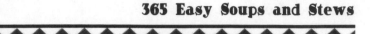

Fresh Oyster Stew

2 pints fresh oysters with liquor	1 kg
3 slices bacon	
1 small onion, chopped	
2 ribs celery, chopped	
1 (4 ounce) can sliced mushrooms	114 g
1 (10 ounce) can cream of potato soup	280 g
3 cups half-and-half cream	710 ml
⅓ cup fresh chopped parsley	80 ml

- Drain oysters and save liquor. Fry bacon until crisp, drain bacon and crumble. Set aside.

- On medium heat in large skillet, cook onion and celery in bacon fat until tender.

- Add mushrooms, soup, oyster liquor, cream and salt and pepper to taste. Heat over medium heat, stirring occasionally, until mixture is thoroughly hot.

- Stir in bacon and oysters and heat 4 to 5 minutes longer or until edges of oysters begin to curl. Sprinkle with parsley.

Fresh chopped parsley added in the last few minutes of cooking adds a wonderful fresh flavor to soups and stews.

Easy New England Clam Chowder

2 (10 ounce) cans New England clam chowder   2 (280 g)
1 (10 ounce) can cream of celery soup   280 g
1 (10 ounce) can cream of potato soup   280 g
1 (10 ounce) can French onion soup   280 g
1 (15 ounce) can cream-style corn   425 g
1 cup whole milk   240 ml

• Combine all ingredients in saucepan. Heat and stir.

Clam Chowder Snap

1 (10 ounce) can New England clam chowder   280 g
1 (10 ounce) can cream of celery soup   280 g
1 (10 ounce) can cream of potato soup   280 g
1 (6.5 ounce) can chopped clams, drained   175 g
1 soup can milk   280 g

• Combine all ingredients in saucepan. Heat and stir.

3-Can Clam Chowder

1 (10 ounce) can New England clam chowder	280 g
1 (10 ounce) can cream of celery soup	280 g
1 (10 ounce) can cream of potato soup	280 g
1 soup can milk	

- Combine all ingredients in saucepan and mix well.

- Heat thoroughly and serve.

Cod and Corn Chowder

8 slices bacon	
1 pound cod, cut into bite-size pieces	.5 kg
2 large baking potatoes, thinly sliced	
3 ribs celery, sliced	
1 onion, chopped	
1 (15 ounce) can whole kernel corn	425 g
1 (8 ounce) carton whipping cream	227 g

- Fry bacon in large, heavy soup pot, remove bacon and drain. Crumble bacon and set aside.

- Drain fat from soup pot and stir in 2½ cups (600 ml) water, cod, potatoes, celery, onion, corn and salt and pepper to taste. Boil, reduce heat, cover and simmer for about 20 minutes or until fish and potatoes are done.

- Stir in cream and heat just until chowder is thoroughly hot. When serving, sprinkle crumbled bacon over each serving.

Crab-Corn Chowder

1 (1.8 ounce) packet dry leek soup mix	57 g
2 cups milk	480 ml
1 (8 ounce) can whole kernel corn, drained	227 g
½ (8 ounce) package cubed processed cheese	½ (227 g)
1 (7 ounce) can crabmeat, flaked	198 g

- Combine soup mix and milk in large saucepan, cook over medium heat and stir constantly until soup begins to thicken. While still on medium heat, stir in corn and cheese and stir until cheese melts.

- Just before serving, add crabmeat and stir until thoroughly hot.

Oyster and Vegetable Chowder

¼ cup (½ stick) butter	60 ml
3 (8 ounce) cans whole oysters with liquor	3 (227 g)
1 (16 ounce) package frozen broccoli florets	.5 kg
1 (10 ounce) package frozen corn	280 g
1 pint half-and-half cream	.5 kg
1 cup milk	240 ml

- Melt butter in large saucepan and stir in oysters, broccoli and corn. Cook over medium heat and stir often for 12 minutes or until vegetables are tender.

- Stir in cream, milk, 1 ½ teaspoons (7 ml) salt and ½ teaspoon (2 ml) pepper. Cook over low heat and stir often until mixture is thoroughly hot.

Seafood Chowder

3 onions, chopped
2 bell peppers, seeded, chopped
2 ribs celery, sliced
¼ cup oil   60 ml
3 tablespoons flour   45 ml
3 (15 ounce) cans stewed tomatoes   3 (425 g)
1 teaspoon minced garlic   5 ml
1 teaspoon hot sauce   5 ml
2 pounds medium fresh shrimp, peeled   1 kg
1 pound fresh lump crabmeat, flaked   .5 kg
1 (12 ounce) carton oysters, drained   340 g

- Saute onions, bell peppers and celery in hot oil in soup pot. Add flour and cook for 1 minute, stirring constantly. Stir in tomatoes, garlic, hot sauce and salt and pepper to taste. Boil, reduce heat and simmer 15 minutes.

- Add shrimp, crabmeat and oysters to soup. Cover and simmer for 15 minutes.

Cauliflower-Crab Chowder

1 (16 ounce) package frozen cauliflower	.5 kg
¼ cup (½ stick) butter	60 ml
¼ cup flour	60m l
1 (14 ounce) can chicken broth	396 g
1 ½ cups milk	360 ml
1 (3 ounce) package cream cheese, cubed	84 g
1 (2 ounce) jar chopped pimiento, drained	57 g
1 teaspoon dried parsley	5 ml
1 (8 ounce) package refrigerated, imitation crabmeat, drained	227 g

- Cook cauliflower in ¾ cup (180 ml) water in large saucepan until tender-crisp.

- In another saucepan, melt butter, stir in flour and mix well. Add broth, milk and cream cheese and cook, stirring constantly, until thick and bubbly.

- Add mixture to saucepan with cauliflower and stir in pimiento, parsley and salt and pepper to taste.

- Stir in crab and heat just until thoroughly hot.

Everybody's Seafood Gumbo

¼ cup (½ stick) butter	60 ml
4 tablespoons flour	60 ml
1 ½ - 2 pounds fresh okra, sliced	.7 kg
2 (15 ounce) cans whole tomatoes	2 (425 g)
½ cup minced onion	120 ml
1 pound shrimp, peeled, cleaned	.5 kg
1 pound crabmeat, flaked, drained	.5 kg
1 pound fish filets, quartered	.5 kg
1 pint fresh oysters with liquor	.5 kg
Rice	

- Melt butter and add flour in heavy skillet. Stir well over medium heat to make smooth, paste-like roux. When roux is rich brown color, add salt and pepper to taste and mix well. Add 2 quarts (2 L) water, okra, tomatoes and onion. Cook on low for 20 minutes.

- Add all seafood and cook on medium to low for 30 minutes or until desired consistency. Serve over rice.

Seafood Gumbo

¼ cup olive oil	60 ml
½ cup flour	120 ml
1 onion, finely chopped	
2 teaspoons minced garlic	10 ml
2 (10 ounce) packages frozen okra	2 (280 g)
1 (15 ounce) can diced tomatoes	425 g
¾ teaspoon cayenne pepper	4 ml
1 pound fresh, peeled, veined shrimp	.5 kg
1 pound crabmeat, flaked, drained	.5 kg
1 pint oysters, drained	.5 kg
3 fresh green onions, sliced	
Hot cooked rice	

- Mix oil and flour in large soup pot. Cook over medium heat and stir constantly until paste-like roux turns light brown. Add onion, garlic, okra and tomatoes and cook on medium heat for about 10 minutes.

- Stir in 1 cup (240 ml) water, 2 teaspoons (10 ml) salt and cayenne pepper and simmer for 25 minutes.

- Add shrimp and crabmeat and simmer for 10 minutes. Add oysters and cook 5 more minutes. Stir in green onions and serve over hot cooked rice.

Super Easy Gumbo

1 (10 ounce) can pepper-pot soup	280 g
1 (10 ounce) can chicken gumbo soup	280 g
1 (6 ounce) can white crabmeat, flaked	168 g
1 (6 ounce) can tiny shrimp, drained	168 g

- Combine all ingredients with 1½ soup cans water in saucepan.

- Cover and simmer for 15 minutes.

Okra Gumbo

1 pound fresh okra, sliced	.5 kg
1 onion, chopped	
½ cup (1 stick) butter	120 ml
1 large potato, peeled, chopped	
2 (15 ounce) cans diced tomato	2 (425 g)
1 (15 ounce) can whole kernel corn	425 g
Hot cooked instant rice	

- Saute okra and onion in butter in soup pot until light brown on outside. Add potato, tomatoes and corn and simmer about 30 minutes or until okra and potatoes are tender. Serve over hot, cooked rice.

Veggie Meatless Masterpieces

The Ultimate Cheddar Cheese Soup

1 cup finely chopped onion	240 ml
1 red bell pepper, diced	
2 tablespoons (¼ stick) butter	30 ml
1 (16 ounce) package shredded extra sharp cheddar cheese	.5 kg
2 tablespoons cornstarch	30 ml
1 (14 ounce) can chicken broth	396 g
1 (10 ounce) package frozen broccoli florets, thawed	280 g
1 (8 ounce) can sliced carrots	168 g
1 teaspoon Worcestershire sauce	5 ml
½ teaspoon garlic powder	2 ml
1 (1 pint) carton half-and-half cream	.5 kg

- Saute onion and bell pepper in butter in large saucepan. Mix cheese and cornstarch in bowl.

- Pour broth and cheese-cornstarch mixture, a little at a time over onion and peppers and heat, stirring constantly, until cheese melts. Stir until smooth and add broccoli, carrots, Worcestershire sauce, ¼ teaspoon (1 ml) each of salt and pepper and garlic powder.

- Simmer and slowly add cream while stirring. Do not boil. Serve immediately.

Old-Time Cheese Soup

¼ cup (½ stick) butter	60 ml
1 small onion, finely chopped	
2 ribs celery, finely chopped	
½ cup shredded carrots	120 ml
¼ cup flour	60 ml
1 tablespoon cornstarch	15 ml
4 cups whole milk	1 L
2 (14 ounce) cans chicken broth	2 (396 g)
1 (12 ounce) package cubed processed cheese	340 g
1 tablespoon dried parsley	15 ml

- Melt butter in heavy saucepan on medium heat and saute onion, celery and carrots about 10 minutes. Stir in flour and cornstarch and cook on low heat until bubbly.

- Gradually stir in milk and broth and blend into a smooth sauce. Add cheese; heat and stir constantly until mixture is smooth. Season with salt and pepper to taste and stir in parsley. Heat, but do not boil.

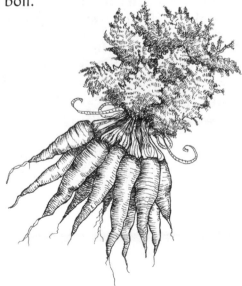

Country Cheddar Cheese Soup

¼ cup (½ stick) butter	60 ml
2 ribs celery, chopped	
1 small onion, finely chopped	
1 bell pepper, seeded, chopped	
1 carrot, shredded	
1 (14 ounce) can chicken broth	396 g
½ cup (1 stick) butter	120 ml
⅔ cup flour	160 ml
1 quart milk	1 L
1 (8 ounce) package shredded sharp cheddar cheese	227 g

- Melt ¼ cup (60 ml) butter and cook celery, onion, bell pepper and carrot in saucepan until tender and stir often. Stir in chicken broth, boil, reduce heat and cook on low heat for 10 minutes.

- While vegetables cook, heat ½ cup (120 ml) butter in large saucepan, stir in flour and cook, stirring constantly, until bubbly.

- Remove from heat and gradually add milk. Cook over medium heat, stirring often, until soup thickens, but do not boil. Stir in cheese and heat until cheese melts. Stir in vegetable-broth mixture and heat just until hot.

Best Ever Cheese Soup

¼ cup (½ stick) butter	60 ml
1 bunch fresh green onions, sliced	
4 ribs celery, sliced	
3 (14 ounce) cans chicken broth	3 (396 g)
2 (10 ounce) cans cream of potato soup	2 (280 g)
1 (12 ounce) package shredded cheddar cheese	340 g
1 (8 ounce) carton sour cream	227 g

- Melt butter in large soup pot and saute onions and celery until tender. Add chick broth and bring to a boil, reduce heat and simmer for 20 minutes.

- Stir in potato soup and cheese and heat, stirring constantly, until cheese melts. Add sour cream and heat. Stir just until sour cream dissolves. Do not boil.

Beer-Cheese Soup

¼ cup (½ stick) butter	60 ml
¼ cup flour	60 ml
1 pint half-and-half cream	.5 kg
1 (12 ounce) can beer (not light)	340 g
1 (16 ounce) package cubed, processed cheese	.5 kg
¼ teaspoon cayenne pepper	1 ml
2 teaspoons white wine Worcestershire sauce	2 ml

- Melt butter and add flour in large soup pot, stir until smooth and cook 1 minute. Gradually add cream and beer and cook over medium heat, stirring constantly, until thick.

- Add cheese and stir until cheese melts. Stir in cayenne pepper, Worcestershire, salt to taste and a dash of hot sauce, if you like. Heat while stirring and ladle into soup bowls.

Incredible Broccoli-Cheese Soup

This really is an incredible soup!

1 (10 ounce) package frozen chopped broccoli	280 g
3 tablespoons butter	45 ml
¼ onion, finely chopped	
¼ cup flour	60 ml
1 (1 pint) carton half-and-half cream	.5 kg
1 (14 ounce) can chicken broth	396 g
⅛ teaspoon cayenne pepper	.5 ml
1 (8 ounce) package mild Mexican-style, cubed,	
processed cheese	227 g

- Punch several holes in broccoli package and microwave for 5 minutes. Turn package in microwave and cook another 4 minutes. Leave in microwave for 3 minutes.

- Melt butter and saute onion in large saucepan, but do not brown. Add flour, stir and gradually add cream, chicken broth, ½ teaspoon (2 ml) salt, ⅛ teaspoon (.5 ml) pepper and cayenne pepper. Stir constantly and heat until mixture is slightly thick. Do not let mixture boil!

- Add cheese, stir constantly and heat until cheese melts. Add cooked broccoli. Serve piping hot.

Creamy Chile-Cheese Soup

½ onion, minced	
1 large tomato, minced	
1 large, fresh green chile, peeled, seeded, minced	
½ clove garlic, minced	
3 tablespoons butter, divided	45 ml
1 (14 ounce) can chicken broth	396 g
2 tablespoons flour	30 ml
3 cups milk, divided	710 ml
1 (12 ounce) package shredded Monterey Jack cheese	340 g

- Saute onion, tomato, green chile and garlic until translucent in large skillet with 1 tablespoon (15 ml) butter. Pour in chicken broth, stir gently and pour into large saucepan.

- Melt 2 tablespoons (30 ml) butter and add flour to skillet, stir constantly until mixture is smooth and beige in color. Stir out any lumps.

- Slowly pour in 1½ cups (360 ml) milk and stir constantly until sauce thickens slightly. Pour mixture into saucepan and continue cooking on simmer.

- Pour in remaining milk, ½ teaspoon (2 ml) salt, ¼ teaspoon (1 ml) pepper and cheese into saucepan and stir constantly. Simmer until cheese melts. Pour into soup cups and serve immediately.

Fiesta Tortilla Soup Con Queso

3 (14 ounce) cans chicken broth	3 (396 g)
2 (15 ounce) cans stewed tomatoes	2 (425 g)
4 green onions with tops, chopped	
1 (7 ounce) cans diced green chilies, drained	198 g
1 clove garlic, minced	
8 corn tortillas	
2 tablespoons oil	30 ml
1 (16 ounce) package cubed Mexican processed cheese	.5 kg

- Pour chicken broth, tomatoes, onions, green chilies and garlic in large saucepan and heat on medium.

- Cut tortillas into long, narrow strips. In skillet with hot oil, fry tortilla strips about 10 seconds or until strips are crisp. Remove from skillet and drain.

- Heat soup to boiling, reduce heat to low and stir in cheese. Serve in individual bowls and garnish with tortilla strips.

Cream of Artichoke Soup

2 shallots, finely chopped	
2 tablespoons butter	30 ml
2 tablespoons flour	30 ml
1 (14 ounce) can chicken broth	396 g
1 ¼ cups artichoke hearts, rinsed, drained, chopped	300 ml
3 tablespoons fresh minced parsley, divided	45 ml
1 ¼ cups half-and-half cream	300 ml

- Saute shallots in saucepan with butter until they are transparent. Add flour, stir to remove lumps and cook.

- Remove from heat and stir in chicken broth, artichoke hearts and 2 tablespoons (30 ml) chopped parsley.

- Return to medium heat and cook for 5 minutes. Puree mixture in blender. Strain pureed mixture through coarse sieve and return to clean saucepan.

- Heat on medium, slowly add cream and blend thoroughly. Serve hot or cold. Garnish with remaining parsley if desired.

Guacamole Soup

1 (18 ounce) can spicy tomato cocktail juice	510 g
½ cup chopped onion	120 ml
2 avocados, peeled, seeded, diced, divided	

- Heat tomato juice and onion in soup pot for 5 minutes or until very hot. Stir in three-fourths of diced avocado and heat.

- Reserve remaining one-fourth avocado for garnish. Sprinkle on top of soup and serve immediately.

Asparagus Soup

¼ cup (½ stick) butter	60 ml
3 (14 ounce) cans chicken broth	3 (396 g)
¾ teaspoon garlic powder	4 ml
1 bunch green onions with tops, diced	
1 large potato, peeled, cubed	
½ (8 ounce) package cubed Velveeta® cheese	½ (227 g)
1 (15 ounce) can extra long asparagus spears	425 g
1 (8 ounce) carton sour cream	227 g
Real bacon bits	

- Combine butter, broth, garlic, green onion and potato in large saucepan. Heat and cook for 15 minutes or until potatoes are tender. Add cheese and heat long enough for cheese to melt.

- Cut asparagus spears into 1-inch (2.5 cm) lengths and add to soup. Fold in sour cream and heat (do not boil) just enough to make soup hot. Sprinkle bacon bits over top of soup before serving. Serves 6 to 8.

TIP: This may be made day before. If you want a spicy soup, use mild Mexican cheese instead of original cheese.

Creamy Asparagus Soup

1 onion, finely chopped	
1 red bell pepper, seeded, chopped	
2 tablespoons butter	30 ml
2 (15 ounce) cans cut asparagus, drained	2 (425 g)
2 (10 ounce) cans cream of chicken soup	2 (280 g)
1 pint half-and-half cream	.5 kg
1 teaspoon lemon juice	5 ml
¼ teaspoon dried tarragon	1 ml

- Saute onion and bell pepper in butter in soup pot. Add asparagus and blend in food processor until smooth.

- Return onion-asparagus mixture to soup pot and add chicken soup, cream, lemon juice, tarragon and salt and pepper to taste. Cook on medium to high heat and stir constantly until soup is thoroughly hot.

At-Home Black Bean Soup

2 onions, finely chopped	
3 teaspoons minced garlic	15 ml
3 (15 ounce) cans black beans, rinsed, drained	3 (425 g)
2 (14 ounce) cans beef broth	2 (396 g)
1 ½ teaspoons dried cumin	7 ml
2 teaspoons chili powder	10 ml
Shredded sharp cheddar cheese	

- Saute onions and garlic in soup pot with a little oil and cook on medium heat for 5 minutes. Place 1 can beans and about ½ cup (120 ml) broth in food processor and process until beans are smooth.

- Transfer to soup pot and stir in remaining beans, remaining broth, cumin, chili powder, salt and pepper to taste. Boil, reduce heat and simmer for 15 minutes.

Black Bean Soup Mix

1 pound dried black beans	.5 kg
1 (32 ounce) carton chicken broth	1 kg
2 onions, chopped	
1 bell pepper, seeded, chopped	
1 tablespoon minced garlic	15 ml
2 tablespoons oil	30 ml
2 (10 ounce) cans tomatoes and green chilies	2 (280 g)
1 teaspoon chili powder	5 ml
⅓ cup lemon juice	80 ml
1 (8 ounce) carton sour cream	227 g

- Sort, rinse beans and place in soup pot. Cover with water 2 inches (5 cm) above beans. Bring beans to boil, cover, remove from heat and let stand 1 hour. Drain beans and return to soup pot.

- Add chicken broth to beans in pot, cover and cook over medium heat for 3 hours or until beans are tender. Stir occasionally. If beans get a little too dry, add ½ to 1 cup (120 ml) water.

- Saute onions, bell pepper and garlic in hot oil in large skillet until tender. Stir in tomatoes and green chilies, chili powder, lemon juice and salt and pepper to taste and cook 5 more minutes.

- In food processor, process 2 cups (480 ml) cooked beans until smooth. Stir in remaining beans in soup kettle and add onion-tomato mixture. Cook just until thoroughly hot, ladle into soup bowls and top each bowl with dollop of sour cream.

Ranchero Black Bean Soup

1 cup dried black beans	240 ml
3 (14 ounce) cans beef broth	3 (396 g)
1 large bunch green onions with tops, chopped	
5 ribs celery, chopped	
3 cloves garlic, minced	
½ cup (1 stick) butter	120 ml
½ cup uncooked rice	120 ml
1 bay leaf	
6 peppercorns	
½ teaspoon cayenne pepper	2 ml

- Sort beans, rinse and soak in water overnight. Drain beans, transfer to large saucepan and cook for about 2 hours in beef broth.

- Saute onions, celery and garlic in butter in skillet until onions are translucent.

- Transfer onions, celery, garlic, rice, bay leaf, peppercorns, 1 teaspoon (5 ml) salt and cayenne pepper to beans.

- Cook another 2 hours or until beans are tender. (Add water if needed.) Remove bay leaf and peppercorns before serving.

TIP: When serving, it is a nice touch to garnish with grated cheese, sour cream or chopped green onions.

Southwestern Bean Soup

Don't let the number of ingredients discourage you. Ask yourself this question,
"Can I open cans?"

¼ cup (½ stick) butter	60 ml
1 onion, chopped	
1 bell pepper, seeded, chopped	
2 teaspoons minced garlic	10 ml
2 (15 ounce) cans Mexican-style stewed	
tomatoes	2 (425 g)
1 (15 ounce) can pinto beans, drained	425 g
1 (15 ounce) can kidney beans, rinsed, drained	425 g
1 (15 ounce) can black beans, rinsed, drained	425 g
1 tablespoon chili powder	15 ml
¼ teaspoon ground coriander	1 ml
1 cup shredded Mexican-style 4-cheese blend	240 ml
1 cup shredded Monterey Jack cheese, divided	240 ml

- Melt butter in large saucepan on medium heat and cook onion, bell pepper and garlic for 5 minutes. Stir in tomatoes, all 3 cans beans, chili powder, coriander and salt and pepper to taste.

- Boil, reduce heat, cover and simmer for 25 minutes.

- Stir in Mexican-style cheese and cook over low heat, stirring occasionally, just until cheese melts.

- Ladle into individual soup bowls and sprinkle Jack cheese over each serving.

Zesty Black Bean Soup

2 onions, finely chopped	
3 teaspoons minced garlic	15 ml
3 teaspoons chili powder	15 ml
3 (15 ounce) cans black beans, divided	3 (425 g)
1 teaspoon cumin	5 ml
1 (14 ounce) can beef broth	396 g

- Saute onions in soup pot with a little oil, cook on medium heat for 5 minutes and stir in garlic and chili powder.

- Puree 1 can beans and add to onion mixture. Add remaining beans, cumin and beef broth. Boil, reduce heat and simmer for 10 minutes. If you like, garnish with shredded cheese or salsa just before serving.

Black Bean-Corn Soup

1 onion, chopped	
3 teaspoons minced garlic	15 ml
1 (28 ounce) can diced tomatoes	794 g
1 (15 ounce) can black beans, rinsed, drained	425 g
1 (10 ounce) package frozen corn	280 ml
½ cup instant rice, cooked	120 ml
1 red bell pepper, seeded, chopped	
1 teaspoon dried cumin	5 ml

• Saute onion and garlic in a little oil in large soup pot for
  about 5 minutes. Stir in tomatoes, beans, corn, rice, bell
  pepper and cumin.

• Cover pot and boil. Reduce heat and simmer for
  15 minutes.

Creamy Broccoli Soup

2 tablespoons butter	30 ml
½ cup chopped onion	120 ml
1 (14 ounce) can cream of broccoli soup	396 g
1 cup milk	240 ml
4 ounces cream cheese, cubed	114 g
1 (8 ounce) package cubed processed cheese	227 g
1 (10 ounce) package frozen chopped broccoli	280 g

• Melt butter in large, heavy soup pot and saute onion for
  5 minutes. Stir in soup, milk and cream cheese. Cook on
  low to medium heat and stir well until cream cheese melts.

• Add processed cheese, chopped broccoli and salt and pepper
  to taste. Cook on low to medium heat for 10 minutes or until
  cheese melts and soup is thoroughly hot.

Garbanzo Bean Soup

2 tablespoons olive oil	30 ml
1 (16 ounce) package frozen chopped onions and peppers	.5 kg
2 teaspoons minced garlic	10 ml
½ teaspoon dried sage	2 ml
1 (15 ounce) can stewed tomatoes	425 g
2 (14 ounce) cans vegetable stock	2 (396 g)
1 (15 ounce) can garbanzo beans, drained	425 g
½ cup elbow macaroni	120 ml
1 teaspoon Italian seasoning	5 ml
1 (5 ounce) package grated parmesan cheese	143 g

- Combine olive oil, onions, peppers and garlic in soup pot and cook, stirring often, on medium heat for 5 minutes or until onions are translucent. Stir in sage, tomatoes, vegetable stock, garbanzo beans and salt and pepper to taste and cook for 10 minutes. Stir in macaroni and Italian seasoning and cook about 15 minutes or until macaroni is al dente (tender, but not overdone). Place about 1 heaping tablespoon (15 ml) parmesan cheese over each serving.

Mexican Bean Soup

1 (15 ounce) can refried beans	425 g
1 (15 ounce) can pinto beans with jalapenos	425 g
1 (8 ounce) can tomato sauce	227 g
½ cup hot salsa	120 ml
1 onion, chopped	
1 bell pepper, seeded, chopped	
2 (14 ounce) cans beef broth	2 (396 g)

- Combine all ingredients plus 1 cup (240 ml) water and mix well. Boil in large soup pot, reduce heat and simmer for 30 minutes.

Broccoli-Cheddar Soup for Two

⅓ cup chopped onion	80 ml
⅓ cup sliced celery	80 ml
¼ cup (½ stick) butter	60 ml
¼ cup flour	60 ml
1 (10 ounce) can chicken broth	280 g
1 ½ cups milk or half-and-half-cream	360 ml
1 (14 ounce) package frozen chopped	
broccoli, thawed, cooked	280 g
⅔ cup shredded cheddar cheese	160 ml

- Saute onion and celery in butter in large saucepan. Stir in flour and salt and pepper to taste. Cook and stir constantly until smooth.

- Add broth and milk and cook, while stirring, until mixture thickens. Add drained broccoli and simmer, stirring constantly, until mixture is thoroughly hot. Remove from heat, add cheese and stir until cheese melts.

At-Home Broccoli Soup

¼ cup (½ stick) butter	60 ml
2 onions, finely chopped	
3 tablespoons flour	45 ml
3 (14 ounce) cans chicken broth	3 (396 g)
1 (16 ounce) package frozen chopped broccoli	.5 kg
1 cup shredded carrots	240 ml
1 (5 ounce) can evaporated milk	143 g

- Melt butter in soup pot and saute onions for 5 to 6 minutes or until golden. Add flour and stir constantly until light brown. Stir in broth and boil, reduce heat and simmer for 10 minutes, stirring constantly.

- Add broccoli and carrots and cook on medium heat for 10 minutes. Stir in evaporated milk and salt and pepper to taste. Heat just until soup is thoroughly hot.

Broccoli-Wild Rice Soup

This is a hardy and delicious soup full of flavor.

1 (6 ounce) package chicken-flavored wild rice mix	168 g
1 (10 ounce) package frozen chopped broccoli, thawed	280 g
2 teaspoons dried minced onion	10 ml
1 (10 ounce) can cream of chicken soup	280 g
1 (8 ounce) package cream cheese, cubed	227 g

- Combine rice, rice seasoning packet and 6 cups (1.5 L) water in large saucepan. Boil, reduce heat, cover and simmer for 10 minutes, stirring once.

- Stir in broccoli and onion and simmer for 5 minutes.

- Stir in soup and cream cheese. Cook and stir until cheese melts.

Cheese-Topped Broccoli Soup

3 (14 ounce) cans chicken broth	3 (396 g)
2 ribs celery, sliced	
1 onion, chopped	
1 medium baking potato, peeled, chopped	
1 (16 ounce) package frozen chopped broccoli	.5 kg
1 pint half-and-half cream	.5 kg
1 (5 ounce) package grated parmesan cheese	143 g

- Combine broth, ½ cup (120 ml) water, celery, onion and chopped potato in large, heavy soup pot.

- Boil, reduce heat and simmer for 20 minutes or until vegetables are tender.

- Stir in broccoli and boil, reduce heat and simmer for 15 minutes. Stir in cream, ¼ teaspoon (1 ml) pepper and salt to taste.

- Heat on medium, stirring constantly, just until soup is thoroughly hot. Ladle into individual soup bowls and sprinkle with parmesan.

Women are more than twice as likely as men to cite soup as a typical lunch (10 percent versus 4 percent).

Cream of Carrot Soup

1 small onion, chopped	
2 tablespoons butter	30 ml
6 carrots, chopped	
2 tablespoons dry white wine	30 ml
2 (14 ounce) cans chicken broth	2 (396 g)
1/8 teaspoon ground nutmeg	.5 ml
1 (8 ounce) carton whipping cream, whipped	227 g

- Saute onion in butter and add carrots, wine, chicken broth, nutmeg, ½ teaspoon (2 ml) pepper and salt to taste in large saucepan. Boil, reduce heat and simmer for 30 minutes or until carrots are tender. Pour half of carrot mixture into blender, cover and blend on medium speed until mixture is smooth. Repeat with remaining mixture. Return to saucepan and heat just until hot. Stir in whipped cream.

Cauliflower-Potato Soup

1 cup instant mashed potato mix	240 ml
½ cup finely chopped scallions, whites only	120 ml
½ teaspoon caraway seeds	2 ml
2 (14 ounce) cans chicken broth	2 (396 g)
1 (16 ounce) package frozen cauliflower florets	.5 kg
1 (8 ounce) package shredded cheddar cheese, divided	227 g

- Combine 1 ½ cups (360 ml) boiling water, dry mashed potatoes, scallions, caraway seeds, 1 ½ teaspoons (7 ml) salt, 1 teaspoon (5 ml) pepper and chicken broth. Boil, reduce heat to medium and simmer for 10 minutes. Stir in cauliflower and cook about 10 minutes or until cauliflower is tender. Stir in half cheddar cheese. Serve in individual soup bowls and sprinkle remaining cheese over top each serving.

Cheesy Cauliflower Soup

1 (16 ounce) package frozen cauliflower florets	.5 kg
2 ribs celery, sliced	
1 carrot, cut into chunks	
1 onion, chopped	
1 tablespoon instant chicken bouillon granules	15 ml
½ teaspoon lemon pepper	2 ml
1 (8 ounce) carton whipping cream	227 g
1 (8 ounce) package shredded Monterey Jack cheese, divided	227 g

- Combine 2 cups (480 ml) water, cauliflower, celery, carrot, onion, chicken bouillon, ½ teaspoon (2 ml) salt and lemon pepper in large, heavy soup pot.

- Cover and cook 1 hour or until vegetables are very tender.

- Pour half mixture into food processor and process until smooth. Repeat with remaining soup mixture. Return to soup pot and stir in cream and about three-fourths of cheese.

- Cook over medium heat, stirring constantly, until cheese melts and mixture is thoroughly hot. Ladle into individual serving bowls and sprinkle remaining cheese over each serving.

Speedy Cauliflower Soup

2 (14 ounce) cans chicken broth	2 (396 g)
1 (10 ounce) can cream of potato soup	280 g
1 (4 ounce) can chopped pimento	114 g
1 (16 ounce) package frozen cauliflower	.5 kg
1 pint half-and-half cream	

- Combine broth, potato soup, pimento and ¾ cup (180 ml) water in large saucepan. Boil, reduce heat and simmer for 10 minutes.

- Stir in cauliflower and cook another 10 minutes. Add cream and heat just until soup is thoroughly hot.

Corn Soup Ole

2 (15 ounce) cans whole kernel corn	2 (425 g)
½ onion, chopped	
2 tablespoons (¼ stick) butter	30 ml
2 tablespoons flour	30 ml
2 (14 ounce) cans chicken broth	2 (396 g)
1 ½ cups half-and-half cream	360 ml
1 (8 ounce) package shredded cheddar cheese	227 g
1 (4 ounce) can chopped green chilies	114 g
Tortilla chips	
Bacon bits	

- Saute corn and onion in butter. Add flour, ½ teaspoon (2 ml) salt and ¼ teaspoon (1 ml) pepper and cook 1 minute. Gradually add broth and cream while on low to medium heat. Cook until it thickens slightly.

- Add cheddar cheese and green chilies. Heat but do not boil. Serve soup in individual bowls and stir in 4 to 5 crumbled, tortilla chips. Garnish with bacon bits.

Creamy Corn Soup

¼ cup (½ stick) butter	60 ml
1 (16 ounce) package frozen onions and bell peppers	.5 kg
1 (16 ounce) package frozen corn	.5 kg
1 (15 ounce) can cream-style corn	425 g
1 (10 ounce) can diced tomatoes and green chilies	280 g
2 (14 ounce) cans chicken broth	2 (396 g)
¼ cup flour	60 ml
1 pint half-and half-cream	

- Melt butter and saute onions and bell peppers in soup pot on medium heat for 5 minutes. Stir in whole kernel corn, cream-style corn, tomatoes and green chilies and chicken broth.

- Boil, reduce heat and simmer for 20 minutes. Mix ¼ cup (60 ml) water with flour and mix until they blend well. Stir into soup and heat, stirring constantly, until soup thickens.

- Stir in cream and heat soup, stirring constantly, just until thoroughly hot.

Quick-and-Easy Corn Soup

2 (15 ounce) cans whole kernel corn	2 (425 g)
1 (10 ounce) can cream of potato soup	280 g
1 (14 ounce) can chicken broth	396 g
1 (8 ounce) carton whipping cream	227 g
⅛ teaspoon cayenne pepper	.5 ml

- Combine corn, potato soup, broth, cream and cayenne pepper in saucepan. Cook on medium heat, stirring often, until thoroughly hot. Garnish, if you like with bacon bits.

Quickie Corny Soup

3 strips bacon
1 small bunch green onions, minced
1 (15 ounce) can cream-style corn   425 g
1 soup can milk

- Fry bacon in large skillet and drain. Add onions to skillet and saute until translucent. Crumble bacon and sprinkle in skillet.

- Add cream-style corn, milk and salt and pepper to taste. Heat almost to boiling, stir often and pour into soup bowls.

  TIP: If you want to add some type of garnish on top of the soup, fry some extra bacon and crumble it over the top or chop the green onion tops and sprinkle them on top. It looks and tastes great.

Welcome Home Soup

2 cups fresh broccoli florets   480 ml
4 - 5 large new potatoes, chopped
1 bunch green onions with tops, chopped
2 (14 ounce) cans chicken broth   2 (280 g)
Sour cream

- Cook vegetables in chicken broth until tender and season with salt and pepper to taste.   Pour into blender and puree. Pour into soup bowls and garnish with dollop of sour cream. Serves 6 to 8.

Cream of Cauliflower Soup

1 onion, chopped	
½ teaspoon garlic powder	2 ml
2 (14 ounce) cans chicken broth	2 (396 g)
1 large cauliflower, cut into small florets	
1 ½ cups whipping cream	360 ml

- Saute onion and garlic powder in a little oil. Stir in broth and boil. Add cauliflower and cook, stirring occasionally, for 15 minutes or until tender.

- Process soup in batches in blender until smooth and return to pan. Stir in cream and add a little salt and pepper. Cook over low heat, stirring often, until thoroughly hot.

Quick Corn Chowder

2 baking potatoes, peeled, diced	
½ cup shredded carrots	120 ml
½ cup finely chopped onion	120 ml
1 (15 ounce) can cream-style corn	425 g
1 (8 ounce) can whole kernel corn	227 g
1 (10 ounce) can cream of celery soup	280 g
1 cup milk	240 ml
1 (8 ounce) package cubed processed cheese	227 g

- Cook potatoes, carrots and onion in 1½ cups (360 ml) water in large saucepan for about 15 minutes or until potatoes are tender; do not drain.

- Stir in cream-style corn, whole kernel corn, soup, milk and salt and pepper to taste. Heat and stir constantly until mixture is thoroughly hot; stir in cheese and serve.

Merry Split Pea Soup

1 (1 pound) package split peas	.5 kg
1 teaspoon dried parsley	5 ml
½ teaspoon garlic salt	2 ml
1 (14 ounce) can chicken broth	280 g
1 ½ cups minced onion	360 ml
1 ¼ cups minced celery	300 ml
¾ cup minced carrots	180 ml

- Soak peas overnight in water. Drain, rinse and pour 2 quarts (2 L) water over beans in large soup pot. Add parsley, garlic salt, chicken broth, onion and ¾ teaspoon (4 ml) pepper.

- Cover and simmer about 1 ½ to 2 hours. Add remaining ingredients and simmer, covered, another 45 minutes.

Italian Minestrone

1 (16 ounce) package frozen onions and bell peppers	.5 kg
3 ribs celery, chopped	
2 teaspoons minced garlic	10 ml
¼ cup (½ stick) butter	60 ml
2 (15 ounce) cans diced tomatoes	2 (425 g)
1 teaspoon dried oregano	5 ml
1 teaspoon dried basil	5 ml
2 (14 ounce) cans beef broth	2 (396 g)
2 (15 ounce) cans kidney beans, drained	2 (425 g)
2 medium zucchini, cut in half lengthwise, sliced	
1 cup uncooked elbow macaroni	240 ml

- Saute onions, bell peppers, celery and garlic in butter for about 2 minutes in soup pot. Add tomatoes, oregano, basil and salt and pepper to taste. Boil, reduce heat and simmer for 15 minutes, stirring occasionally.

- Stir in beef broth, beans, zucchini and macaroni and boil. Reduce heat and simmer another 15 minutes or until macaroni is tender.

Minestrone soup comes from the Italian word "minestra," which means minister. Clergy ministered to the poor by providing bowls of broth containing potatoes, corn, zucchini, tomatoes, peppers and kidney beans.

Mexican-Style Minestrone Soup

1 (16 ounce) package frozen garlic-seasoned pasta and vegetables	.5 kg
1 (16 ounce) jar thick and chunky salsa	.5 kg
1 (15 ounce) can pinto beans with liquid	425 g
1 teaspoon chili powder	5 ml
1 teaspoon cumin	5 ml
1 (8 ounce) package shredded Mexican 4-cheese blend	227 g

- Combine pasta and vegetables with salsa, beans, chili powder, cumin and 1 cup (240 ml) water in large saucepan. Boil, reduce heat, simmer for about 8 minutes and stir occasionally.

- When ready to serve, top each serving with Mexican cheese.

Mushroom Soup

1 (10 ounce) can cream of mushroom soup	280 g
1 (14 ounce) can sliced mushrooms, drained	396 g
1 (14 ounce) can beef broth	396 g
1 (8 ounce) carton whipping cream	227 g

- Combine all ingredients in medium saucepan.

- Mix well and heat thoroughly.

Creamy Mushroom Soup

3 (8 ounce) packages fresh mushrooms	3 (227 g)
1 small onion, finely chopped	
¼ cup (½ stick) butter, melted	60 ml
½ cup flour	120 ml
2 (14 ounce) cans chicken broth	2 (396 g)
1 pint half-and-half cream	.5 kg
1 (8 ounce) carton whipping cream	227 g
¼ cup dry white wine	60 ml
1 teaspoon dried tarragon	5 ml
2 teaspoons white wine Worcestershire sauce	10 ml

- Coarsely chop and saute mushrooms and onion in butter in large soup pot. Add flour and stir until smooth.

- Add broth, both creams, wine, tarragon, Worcestershire and about 1 teaspoon (5 ml) salt and stir constantly. Boil, reduce heat to medium and cook for 20 minutes or until mixture thickens. Stir often.

Lunch-Ready Mushroom Soup

2 tablespoons butter	30 ml
2 tablespoons flour	30 ml
1 (14 ounce) can chicken broth	396 g
1 cup milk	240 ml
1 (8 ounce) package fresh mushrooms, sliced	227 g
1 teaspoon minced garlic	5 ml
1 teaspoon dried parsley	5 ml
1 teaspoon lemon juice	5 ml
1 cup half-and-half cream	240 ml

- Melt butter, stir in flour in large saucepan and cook, stirring constantly for 1 minute.

- Gradually stir in broth and milk, stirring constantly, and bring to a boil. Add mushrooms, garlic, parsley, lemon juice and salt and pepper to taste and simmer for 5 minutes.

- Add cream and heat just until soup is thoroughly hot; do not boil.

Microwave Mushroom Soup

1 (10 ounce) can cream of mushroom soup	280 g
1 (14 ounce) can beef broth	280 g
1 (4 ounce) can sliced mushrooms, drained	114 g

- Combine mushroom soup and broth in 2-quart (2 L) bowl and mix well. Microwave on HIGH for 1 minute and stir.

- Add sliced mushrooms and mix. Reduce heat to medium and microwave 1 minute longer or until hot. Stir before serving.

Favorite Onion Soup

8 yellow onions, thinly sliced
¼ cup (½ stick) butter   60 ml
2 (32 ounce) cartons beef broth   2 (1 kg)
8 slices French bread, crust trimmed, toasted
8 slices Swiss cheese

- Place onions and butter in large soup pot and saute onions until golden brown. Add beef broth and cook on medium heat for 1 hour.

- Just before time to serve, pour soup into 6 to 8 individual, ovenproof soup bowls, top with slices of toasted bread and cover with slices of cheese.

- Place bowls on baking sheet and place under broiler for 1 to 2 minutes or until cheese melts. Serve immediately.

Easy Veggie Soup

2 (14 ounce) cans beef broth   2 (396 g)
½ cup diced celery   120 ml
1 (16 ounce) can mixed vegetables   .5 kg
1 bay leaf

- Mix all ingredients in large soup pot. Add 1½ cups (360 ml) water, 1 teaspoon (5 ml)each of salt and pepper and simmer for 45 minutes. Adjust seasonings, remove bay leaf and serve.

Tomato-French Onion Soup

1 (10 ounce) can tomato-bisque soup	280 g
2 (10 ounce) cans French-onion soup	2 (280 g)
Croutons	
Grated parmesan cheese	

- Combine soups and 2 soup cans water in saucepan. Heat thoroughly.

- Serve in bowls topped with croutons and sprinkle of cheese.

Winter Sweet Potato Soup

2 tablespoons butter	30 ml
1 cup sliced scallions, whites only	240 ml
2 (15 ounce) cans sweet potatoes with liquid	2 (425 g)
2 (14 ounce) cans chicken broth	2 (396 g)
¼ teaspoon ground cinnamon	1 ml
½ cup half-and-half cream	120 ml

- Melt butter in large saucepan and saute scallions for about 5 minutes. Mash sweet potatoes slightly with fork and place in saucepan with scallions.

- Add chicken broth, cinnamon and salt to taste. Boil and simmer for 5 minutes. Stir in cream.

- Soup may be served warm or chilled.

Creamy Green Pea Soup

1 (16 ounce) package frozen green peas	.5 kg
1 cup milk	240 ml
1 (10 ounce) can cream of chicken soup	280 g
1 (14 ounce) can chicken broth	280 g
1 cup half-and-half cream	240 ml
Shredded Swiss cheese	

- Cook peas according to package directions, place peas and milk in blender and blend to uniform consistency.

- Stir in soup, broth, ½ teaspoon (2 ml) pepper and salt to taste. Bring to boiling (but do not boil), stirring constantly, reduce heat and simmer for 2 minutes.

- Stir in cream and heat soup just until thoroughly hot. Sprinkle cheese over top of each serving.

Luncheon Pea Soup

1 cup instant mashed potato flakes	240 ml
½ cup Italian salad dressing	120 ml
1 (16 ounce) package frozen peas and	
pearl onion	.5 kg
2 (14 ounce) cans chicken broth	2 (396 g)
½ cup sour cream	120 ml

- Heat 1 ¼ cups (300 ml) water, stir in potato flakes in large saucepan and cook for 10 minutes. Stir in salad dressing, peas and onions.

- Transfer soup mixture to blender. Cover and blend small batches until smooth. Return blended mixture to saucepan and add chicken broth and ¾ teaspoon (4 ml) pepper. Boil, reduce heat and simmer about 15 minutes, stirring often. Stir in sour cream.

Creamy Parsley Soup

1 ½ pounds zucchini, chopped	.7 kg
2 (14 ounce) cans chicken broth	2 (396 g)
2 cups loosely packed parsley	
1 (8 ounce) carton whipping cream	227 g

- Combine zucchini and chicken broth in soup pot and cook until tender. Add parsley and cook 5 minutes longer.

- Process in blender until smooth. Return to soup pot over low heat and slowly stir in cream. Season with a little salt and pepper.

TIP: If you need something a little different, substitute watercress for parsley in this recipe. It's wonderful.

Cream of Peanut Soup

½ cup (1 stick) butter	120 ml
1 onion, chopped	
1 red bell pepper, seeded, chopped	
3 ribs celery, finely sliced	
¼ cup flour	60 ml
2 (14 ounce) cans chicken broth	2 (396 g)
1 ½ cups creamy peanut butter	360 ml
1 (1 pint) carton half-and-half cream	.5 kg
1 cup milk	240 ml

- Melt butter and saute onion, bell pepper and celery in large saucepan until vegetables are tender. Add flour, stir until smooth and cook for 1 minute.

- Gradually add chicken broth, stir occasionally, and cook on low heat for 25 minutes. Stir in peanut butter, ½ teaspoon (2 ml) pepper and salt to taste. Gradually add cream and milk, stir constantly and cook over low heat for 5 minutes or until thoroughly hot. Do not boil.

Quick-and-Easy Peanut Soup

¼ cup (½ stick) butter	60 ml
1 onion, finely chopped	
2 ribs celery, chopped	
2 (10 ounce) cans cream of chicken soup	2 (280 g)
2 soup cans milk	
1 ¼ cups crunchy peanut butter	300 ml

- Melt butter in saucepan and saute onion and celery over low heat. Blend in soups and milk and stir.

- Add peanut butter, continue to heat and stir until mixture blends well.

Garlic-Potato Soup

4 cups milk	1 L
1 (7 ounce) package roasted-garlic instant mashed potatoes	198 g
1 (10 ounce) can cream of celery soup	280 g
1 (8 ounce) package shredded sharp cheddar cheese, divided	227 g
1 (4 ounce) can chopped pimento	114 g

- Combine milk and 3 cups (710 ml) water in soup pot and bring to a boil. Remove from heat, add instant potato mix and stir with wire whisk until they mix well. Stir in celery soup and mix well.

- Stir in half cheese, pimento and ½ teaspoon (2 ml) pepper and stir until cheese melts. Ladle into individual bowls and sprinkle remaining cheese on top of each serving.

Easy Potato Soup

1 (18 ounce) package frozen hash brown potatoes	510 g
1 cup chopped onion	240 ml
1 (14 ounce) can chicken broth	396 g
1 (10 ounce) can cream of celery soup	280 g
1 (10 ounce) can cream of chicken soup	280 g
2 cups milk	480 ml

- Combine potatoes, onion and 2 cups (480 ml) water in large saucepan and boil.

- Cover, reduce heat and simmer for 30 minutes. Stir in broth, soups and milk and heat thoroughly.

EZ Potato-Pepper Soup

1 (18 ounce) package frozen hash brown potatoes with onions and peppers	510 g
1 sweet red bell pepper, seeded, chopped	
2 (14 ounce) cans chicken broth	2 (396)
1 (10 ounce) can cream of celery soup	280 g
1 (10 ounce) can cream of chicken soup	280 g
1 (8 ounce) carton whipping cream	227 g
4 fresh green onions, chopped	

- Combine potatoes, bell pepper, chicken broth and 1 cup (240 ml) water in large saucepan and bring to a boil. Cover, reduce heat and simmer 25 minutes.

- Stir in both soups and whipping cream and stir well. Cook until thoroughly hot. Garnish with green onions.

TIP: *If you like, garnish with shredded cheddar cheese or diced, cooked ham.*

Baked Potato Soup

5 large baking potatoes	
¾ cup (1 ½ sticks) butter	180 ml
⅔ cup flour	160 ml
6 cups milk	1.5 L
1 (8 ounce) package shredded cheddar cheese, divided	227 g
1 (3 ounce) package real bacon bits	84 g
1 bunch fresh green onions, chopped, divided	
1 (8 ounce) carton sour cream	227 g

- Cook potatoes in microwave or bake 1 hour at 400° (204° C). Cut potatoes in half lengthwise, scoop out flesh and save. Discard potato shells.

- Melt butter in large soup pot over low heat, add flour and stir until smooth. Gradually add milk and cook over medium heat, stirring constantly, until mixture thickens.

- Stir in potatoes, half cheese, bacon bits, 2 tablespoons (30 ml) green onions and salt and pepper to taste. Cook until hot, but do no boil.

- Stir in sour cream and cook just until hot. Spoon into soup bowls and sprinkle remaining cheese and green onions over each serving.

Leek-Potato Soup

2 pounds baking potatoes, peeled, cubed	1 kg
2 (14 ounce) cans chicken broth	2 (396 g)
¼ cup (½ stick) butter	60 ml
3 ribs celery, thinly sliced	
¾ cup thinly sliced leeks, white only	180 ml
1 (1 pint) carton half-and-half cream	.5 kg
¼ teaspoon ground nutmeg	1 ml

- Combine potatoes and chicken broth in soup pot. Boil, reduce heat and simmer for 10 to 15 minutes or until potatoes are tender. Do not drain. Transfer half potato mixture to blender and blend until smooth. Repeat with remaining potato mixture and return to soup pot.

- Melt butter and cook celery and leeks in saucepan for about 5 minutes or until tender. Spoon into soup pot and add cream, nutmeg, salt and pepper to taste. Heat, stirring constantly, just until mixture is thoroughly hot.

Potato-Cheese Soup

4 large potatoes, peeled, cubed
2 carrots, sliced
2 ribs celery, sliced
1 onion, finely grated
¼ cup (½ stick) butter   60 ml
3 tablespoons instant chicken bouillon granules 45 ml
¼ teaspoon ground thyme   1 ml
½ teaspoon crushed rosemary   2 ml
¼ teaspoon garlic powder   1 ml
2 (1 pint) cartons half-and-half cream   480 ml
1 ½ cups shredded cheddar cheese   360 ml
3 slices bacon, cooked, crumbled

- Cook potatoes and carrots with enough water to cover vegetables in large saucepan. When done, mash with potato masher or mixer, but do not drain water off. Carrots will be chunky.

- Saute celery and onion in butter in small saucepan and add to mashed potatoes in large saucepan. Add all remaining ingredients except bacon and heat just until cheese melts. Lower heat, season with salt and pepper to taste and simmer for 10 minutes.

- Serve with bacon pieces sprinkled over individual bowls of soup.

Pumpkin Soup

1 (8 ounce) package fresh mushrooms, sliced	227 g
3 tablespoons butter	45 ml
¼ cup flour	60 ml
2 (14 ounce) cans vegetable broth	2 (396 g
1 (15 ounce) can cooked pumpkin	425 g
1 (1 pint) carton half-and-half cream	.5 kg
2 tablespoons honey	30 ml
2 tablespoons sugar	30 ml
½ teaspoon curry powder	2 ml
¼ teaspoon ground nutmeg	1 ml

- Saute mushrooms in butter in large saucepan. Add flour, stir well and gradually add broth. Boil and cook for 2 minutes or until mixture thickens.

- Stir in pumpkin, cream, honey, sugar, curry powder and nutmeg. Stir constantly until soup is thoroughly hot.

  TIP: If you have some sour cream, a dollop of sour cream on top of soup is a very nice garnish.

Spinach Soup

2 (10 ounce) packages frozen chopped spinach,	
cooked	2 (280 g)
2 (10 ounce) cans cream of mushroom soup	2 (280 g)
1 cup half-and-half cream	240 ml
1 (14 ounce) can chicken broth	396 g

- Puree spinach, mushroom soup and half-and-half cream in blender in batches.

- Place spinach mixture and chicken broth in saucepan and heat on medium until thoroughly hot.

- Reduce heat to low and simmer for 10 minutes. Serve hot or cold.

Quick Spinach-Rice Soup

3 (14 ounce) cans chicken broth	3 (396 g)
2 (12 ounce) packages frozen creamed spinach,	
thawed	2 (340 g)
1 (10 ounce) can cream of onion soup	280 g
1 (4 ounce) can chopped pimento	114 g
½ cup instant rice	120 ml

- Combine broth, spinach, soup, pimento, rice, salt and pepper to taste in soup pot. Boil, reduce heat and simmer for 10 minutes.

Creamy Butternut Soup

4 cups cooked, mashed butternut squash	1 L
2 (14 ounce) cans chicken broth	2 (396 g)
½ teaspoon sugar	2 ml
1 (8 ounce) carton whipping cream, divided	227 g
¼ teaspoon ground nutmeg	1 ml

• Combine mashed squash, broth, sugar and a little salt in saucepan. Boil and gradually stir in half of whipping cream. Cook until thoroughly hot. Beat remaining whipping cream. When ready to serve, place dollop of whipped cream on soup and sprinkle with nutmeg.

TIP: It takes about 3 to 4 butternut squash to yield 4 cups (1 L).

Zesty Squash Soup

2 tablespoons butter	30 ml
1 onion, finely chopped	
2 tablespoons flour	30 ml
2 (16 ounce) packages frozen yellow squash, thawed	2 (.5 kg)
1 (32 ounce) carton chicken broth	1 kg
1 (7 ounce) can chopped green chilies	198 g
¾ cup whipping cream	180 ml

• Melt butter and saute onion in large soup pot for 3 minutes, stirring constantly. Stir in flour and cook for 1 minute.

• Add yellow squash, broth, ½ cup (120 ml) water, green chilies and salt and pepper to taste. Boil, reduce heat and simmer for 25 minutes.

• Puree soup in batches in blender until mixture is smooth. Return pureed soup to pot, add whipping cream and heat just until soup is thoroughly hot.

Johnny Appleseed's Squash Soup

1 small butternut squash	
3 tart green apples	
1 medium onion, chopped	
¼ teaspoon dried rosemary	1 ml
¼ teaspoon dried marjoram	1 ml
3 (14 ounce) cans chicken broth	3 (396 g)
2 slices white bread	
¼ cup whipping cream	60 ml

- Cut butternut squash in half and scoop out seeds. Peel, core and chop apples. Combine all ingredients except cream in large saucepan. Boil, reduce heat and simmer uncovered for 45 minutes.

- Remove butternut squash, scoop out pulp from peel and discard peel. Add pulp back to mixture and puree in blender until smooth. Return mixture to saucepan and boil. Just before serving, mix in cream.

  TIP: By adding a bit more cream, this soup also tastes great cold.

Cream of Zucchini Soup

1 pound fresh zucchini, grated	.5 kg
1 onion, chopped	
1 (14 ounce) can chicken broth	396 g
½ teaspoon sweet basil	2 ml
2 cups half-and-half cream, divided	480 ml

- Combine zucchini, onion, broth, basil and a little salt and pepper in saucepan. Bring to a boil and simmer until soft. Place in food processor and puree. Gradually add ½ cup (120 ml) cream and blend.

- Return zucchini mixture to saucepan and add remaining cream. Heat, but do not boil.

Zesty Zucchini Soup

¼ cup (½ stick) butter	60 ml
3 cups coarsely chopped zucchini	710 ml
2 ribs celery, thinly sliced	
1 ½ teaspoons Italian seasoning	7 ml
½ - 1 teaspoon curry powder	2 ml
1 (10 ounce) can cream of potato soup	280 g
1 (10 ounce) can French onion soup	280 g
2 cups milk	480 ml

- Melt butter in soup pot and cook on low to medium heat. Add zucchini, celery, Italian seasoning and curry powder; cook and stir constantly for 5 minutes.

- Stir in potato soup, onion soup and milk. Boil, reduce heat and simmer about 10 minutes.

TIP: *If you want to serve with a nice garnish, place croutons and chopped green onions on top.*

Homemade Tomato Soup

3 (15 ounce) cans whole tomatoes with liquid	3 (425 g)
1 (14 ounce) can chicken broth	396 g
1 tablespoon sugar	15 ml
1 tablespoon minced garlic	15 ml
1 tablespoon balsamic vinegar	15 ml
¾ cup whipping cream	180 ml

- Puree tomatoes in batches with blender and pour into large saucepan. Add chicken broth, sugar, garlic, balsamic vinegar and a little salt. Bring to a boil, reduce heat and simmer for 15 minutes.

- Pour in whipping cream, stir constantly and heat until soup is thoroughly hot.

  TIP: *If you want to fry some bacon or have some ready-cooked, crumbled bacon in the pantry, it would be great as a garnish. If you don't have time, don't worry about it. No one will miss it, if you don't use it.*

Tomato-Basil Soup

2 (10 ounce) cans tomato soup	2 (280 g)
1 (15 ounce) can diced tomatoes	425 g
2 teaspoons finely minced onion	10 ml
2 ½ cups buttermilk*	600 ml
2 tablespoons chopped fresh basil	30 ml

- Combine tomato soup, tomatoes, onion, buttermilk, basil and ¼ teaspoon (1 ml) pepper and salt to taste in saucepan. Cook, stirring often, for 8 minutes or until thoroughly hot.

  *TIP: *To make buttermilk, mix 1 cup milk with 1 tablespoon lemon juice or vinegar and let milk rest about 10 minutes.*

Creamy Tomato Soup

¼ cup (½ stick) butter	60 ml
1 onion, chopped	
2 (28 ounce) cans diced tomatoes with liquid, drained	2 (794 g)
2 tablespoons light brown sugar	30 ml
2 tablespoons tomato paste	30 ml
2 tablespoons flour	30 ml
1 (14 ounce) can chicken broth	396 g
1 (8 ounce) carton whipping cream	227 g

- Melt butter in large soup pot, saute onions about 4 minutes and stir constantly.

- Add drained tomatoes, brown sugar and mixture of tomato paste and flour. Cook, stirring often, on medium heat for 10 minutes. Gradually stir in broth and reserved tomato juice and simmer on low for 15 minutes.

- Puree soup in batches in food processor until mixture is smooth. Pour pureed mixture back into soup pot and heat to boiling.

- Immediately remove from heat. Stir in whipping cream and salt to taste.

TIP: If you want a "snappy" soup with a little fire, just add some hot sauce or a little cayenne pepper. That will get their attention.

Andy Warhol said he painted soup cans because he had soup for lunch every day for 20 years.

Tomato-Ravioli Soup

1 (15 ounce) can stewed tomatoes	425 g
2 (14 ounce) cans chicken broth	2 (396 g)
¾ teaspoon dried Italian seasoning	4 ml
1 (12 ounce) carton fresh cheese ravioli	340 g
2 small zucchini, sliced	
4 fresh green onions, sliced	

- Combine tomatoes, chicken broth, ½ teaspoon (2 ml) pepper and Italian seasoning in large saucepan. Boil, reduce heat and simmer for 5 minutes.

- Add ravioli and zucchini and boil, reduce and simmer for 8 to 10 minutes or until ravioli are tender. Sprinkle a few sliced green onions over each individual serving.

Warm-Your-Soul Soup

3 (14 ounce) cans chicken broth	3 (425 g)
1 (15 ounce) can Italian-stewed tomatoes with liquid	280 g
½ cup chopped onion	120 ml
¾ cup chopped celery	180 ml
½ (12 ounce) box fettuccine	½ (340 g)

- Combine chicken broth, tomatoes, onion and celery in large soup pot. Boil and simmer until onion and celery are almost done.

- Add pasta and cook al dente (firm but tender). Season with little salt and pepper.

Fiesta Soup

1 (15 ounce) can Mexican-style stewed tomatoes	425 g
1 (15 ounce) can whole kernel corn	425 g
1 (15 ounce) can pinto beans with liquid	425 g
2 (14 ounce) cans chicken broth	2 (396 g)
1 (10 ounce) can fiesta nacho cheese soup	280 g

- Combine tomatoes, corn, pinto beans, broth and a little salt and mix well.

- Stir in soup and heat until thoroughly hot.

  TIP: *If you want a heartier soup, just add 1 (12 ounce/340 g) can white chicken chunks.*

El Paso Tomato Soup

2 (10 ounce) cans tomato soup	2 (280 g)
1 (14 ounce) can chopped Mexican stewed tomatoes with onions	396 g
1 (10 ounce) can chopped tomatoes and green chilies	280 g

- Mix all ingredients plus 1 soup can water in saucepan.

- Heat to boiling and stir often. Reduce heat and simmer for 5 minutes.

Zippy Tomato Soup

2 tablespoons butter	30 ml
1 onion, chopped	
2 ribs celery, sliced	
1 bell pepper, seeded, chopped	
1 teaspoon minced garlic	5 ml
2 (15 ounce) cans Italian stewed tomatoes	2 (425 g)
1 (14 ounce) can vegetable stock	396 g
½ teaspoon cayenne pepper	2 ml
⅓ cup sour cream	80 ml

- Melt butter and cook onion, celery, bell pepper and garlic in large saucepan over medium heat, for 10 minutes or until vegetables are tender, but not brown.

- Stir in stewed tomatoes and transfer, in batches, to food processor. Process until soup is almost smooth.

- Return soup mixture to saucepan and add vegetable stock, cayenne pepper, salt and pepper to taste. Heat for 5 minutes or until soup is thoroughly hot and stir in sour cream just before serving.

TIP: If you have some croutons in the pantry, throw a couple on top of each soup bowl before you serve. It's a nice touch, but not a "must-do".

Tomato-Tortilla Soup

8 corn tortillas, cut into strips	
Oil	
1 onion, chopped	
½ cup finely chopped green bell pepper	120 ml
½ teaspoon ground cumin	2 ml
2 teaspoons minced garlic	10 ml
2 (15 ounce) cans diced tomatoes	2 (425 g)
1 (4 ounce) can chopped green chilies	114 g
3 (14 ounce) cans chicken broth	3 (396 g)
½ bunch fresh cilantro, very finely chopped	
1 (8 ounce) package shredded cheddar cheese	227 g

- Fry tortilla strips in hot oil and drain on paper towels.

- Saute onion, bell pepper, cumin and garlic in 2 tablespoons (30 ml) oil in large heavy soup pot.

- Add diced tomatoes, green chilies, chicken broth and cilantro and stir occasionally. Cook for 20 to 25 minutes.

- When ready to serve, place some tortilla strips and shredded cheese in each bowl, pour soup into bowls and serve immediately.

  TIP: *If you want to make this a hearty, one-dish meal, add 2 cups (480 ml) cooked, chopped chicken breasts.*

Cheesy Vegetable Soup

2 large potatoes, peeled, diced	
1 (16 ounce) package frozen onions and peppers	.5 kg
2 (14 ounce) cans chicken broth	2 (396 g)
1 (4 ounce) can sliced mushrooms, drained	114 g
1 (16 ounce) package frozen mixed vegetables	.5 kg
1 (10 ounce) can cream of celery soup	280 g
1 (12 ounce) package cubed Velveeta® cheese	340 g

- Combine potatoes, onions, peppers, chicken broth and 2 cups (480 ml) water in large soup pot on medium heat. Cook for 15 to 20 minutes or until potatoes are tender.

- Stir in mushrooms, mixed vegetables and 1 teaspoon (5 ml) salt and cook another 10 minutes.

- Stir in celery soup and cheese, heat on low to medium and stir until cheese melts.

Swiss-Vegetable Soup

1 (1 ounce) packet dry vegetable soup mix	28 g
1 cup half-and-half cream	240 ml
1 ½ cups shredded Swiss cheese	360 ml

- Combine soup mix and 3 cups (710 ml) water in saucepan and boil.

- Lower heat and simmer about 10 minutes. Add cream and cheese, stir and serve hot.

Spicy Tomato Soup

2 (10 ounce) cans tomato soup	2 (280 g)
1 (15 ounce) can Mexican stewed tomatoes	425 g
1 (4 ounce) can chopped green chilies	114 g
1 (10 ounce) can French onion soup	280 g
3 slices bacon, fried, drained, crumbled	

- Combine tomato soup, stewed tomatoes, green chilies and onion soup in saucepan and heat thoroughly.

- To serve, sprinkle crumbled bacon on top.

Southwest Chili and Tomatoes

4 scallions, sliced	
4 teaspoons minced garlic	20 ml
2 teaspoons olive oil	10 ml
2 (15 ounce) cans diced tomatoes with liquid	2 (425 g)
1 (15 ounce) can pinto beans, rinsed, drained	425 g
¾ teaspoon cayenne pepper	4 ml
2 tablespoons chili powder	30 ml
1 teaspoon ground cumin	5 ml
½ teaspoon coriander	2 ml
6 fresh sage leaves, snipped	

- Saute scallions and garlic with olive oil in large saucepan over medium heat for about 3 minutes. Add tomatoes, beans, cayenne pepper, chili powder, cumin, coriander and salt to taste.

- Heat chili to boiling, reduce heat, add sage and cook uncovered for 2 minutes. Remove sage leaves before serving.

Favorite Veggie-Lovers' Chili

2 onions, coarsely chopped	
2 tablespoons olive oil	30 ml
2 (14 ounce) cans diced tomatoes	2 (396 g)
⅔ cup medium-hot salsa	160 ml
2 teaspoons ground cumin	10 ml
½ teaspoon dried oregano	2 ml
2 (15 ounce) cans pinto beans	2 (425 g)
1 green and 1 red bell pepper, coarsely chopped	
1 cup halved baby carrots	240 ml
4 cups hot cooked rice	1 L
1 (8 ounce) package shredded cheddar cheese	227 g

- Saute onion in oil in large soup pot. Add ½ cup (120 ml) water, tomatoes, salsa, cumin, oregano and salt and pepper to taste. Boil, reduce heat and simmer for 10 minutes.

- Stir in beans, bell peppers and carrots. Cover and cook over medium heat for 25 minutes and stir occasionally.

- Spoon rice into individual soup bowls and ladle chili over rice. Sprinkle generous amount of cheddar cheese on top of soup.

Ninety-nine percent of all American households purchase soup each year, making it a $5 billion business.

Vegetarian Chili

2 (15 ounce) cans stewed tomatoes	2 (425 g)
1 (15 ounce) can kidney beans, rinsed, drained	425 g
1 (15 ounce) can pinto beans with liquid	425 g
1 onion, chopped	
1 green bell pepper, chopped	
1 tablespoon chili powder	15 ml
1 (12 ounce) package elbow macaroni	340 g
¼ cup (½ stick) butter, sliced	60 ml

- Combine tomatoes, kidney beans, pinto beans, onion, bell pepper, chili powder and 1 cup (240 ml) water in soup pot. Cover and cook on medium heat for 1 hour.

- Cook macaroni according to package directions, drain and add butter. Stir until butter melts. Add macaroni to chili and mix well.

Supper-Ready Vegetable Chili

1 (28 ounce) can diced tomatoes	794 g
1 (16 ounce) jar thick, chunky salsa	.5 kg
1 (15 ounce) can black beans, rinsed, drained	425 g
1 (15 ounce) can pinto beans, drained	425 g
1 (8 ounce) can whole kernel corn	227 g
1 tablespoon chili powder	15 ml
1 (8 ounce) package shredded cheddar cheese	227 g

- Combine tomatoes, salsa, black beans, pinto beans, corn and chili powder in large soup pot. Boil, reduce heat and simmer for 15 minutes and stir often.

- Before serving, sprinkle 2 or 3 tablespoons (30 ml) cheese over top of each serving.

Slow
Cooker

Chicken and Rice Soup

1 (6 ounce) package long grain-wild rice mix	168 g
1 (1 ounce) packet chicken-noodle soup mix	28 g
2 (10 ounce) cans cream of chicken soup	2 (280 g)
2 ribs celery, chopped	
2 cups cooked, cubed chicken	480 ml

- Combine all ingredients and about 6 cups (1.5 L) water in 5 to 6-quart (5 L) slow cooker. Stir soup to mix. Cover and cook on LOW for 2 to 3 hours.

Tasty Chicken and Rice Soup

1 pound boneless, skinless chicken breast halves	.5 kg
½ cup brown rice	120 ml
1 (10 ounce) can cream of chicken soup	280 g
1 (10 ounce) can cream of celery soup	280 g
1 (14 ounce) can chicken broth with roasted garlic	396 g
1 (16 ounce) package frozen, sliced carrots, thawed	.5 kg
1 cup half-and-half cream	240 ml

- Cut chicken into 1-inch (2.5 cm) pieces. Place pieces in sprayed 4 or 5-quart (4 L) slow cooker.

- Mix rice, both soups, chicken broth and carrots in saucepan, heat just enough to mix well and pour over chicken. Cover and cook on LOW for 7 to 8 hours.

- Turn heat to HIGH, add cream and cook another 15 to 20 minutes.

Chicken and Barley Soup

1 ½ - 2 pounds boneless, skinless chicken thighs	.7 kg
1 (16 ounce) package frozen stew vegetables	.5 kg
1 (1 ounce) packet dry vegetable soup mix	28 g
1 ¼ cups pearl barley	300 ml
2 (14 ounce) cans chicken broth	2 (396 g)

- Combine all ingredients plus 1 teaspoon (5 ml) each of salt and pepper and 4 cups (1 L) water in large, sprayed slow cooker.

- Cover and cook on LOW for 5 to 6 hours or on HIGH for 3 hours.

Creamy Chicken Soup

2 cups milk	480 ml
1 (7 ounce) package cheddar-broccoli soup starter	198 g
1 cup cooked, finely chopped chicken breasts	240 ml
1 (10 ounce) package frozen green peas, thawed	280 g
Shredded cheddar cheese	

- Place 5 cups (1.5 L) water and milk in slow cooker. Set heat on HIGH until water and milk come to boil.

- Stir contents of soup starter into hot water and milk and stir well. Add chopped chicken, green peas and a little salt and pepper.

- Cook on LOW for 2 to 3 hours.

- To serve, sprinkle cheddar cheese over each serving of soup.

Confetti-Chicken Soup

1 pound boneless, skinless chicken thighs	.5 kg
1 (6 ounce) package chicken and herb-flavored rice	168 g
3 (14 ounce) cans chicken broth	3 (396 g)
3 carrots, sliced	
1 (10 ounce) can cream of chicken soup	280 g
1 ½ tablespoons chicken seasoning	22 ml
1 (10 ounce) package frozen corn, thawed	280 g
1 (10 ounce) package frozen baby green peas, thawed	280 g

- Cut thighs in thin strips.

- Combine chicken, rice, chicken broth, carrots, soup, chicken seasoning and 1 cup (240 ml) water in 5 or 6-quart (5 L) slow cooker.

- Cover and cook on LOW for 8 to 9 hours.

- About 30 minutes before serving, turn heat to HIGH and add corn and peas to cooker. Continue cooking for another 30 minutes.

If you have any leftover cooked pasta, meat or vegetables, use them for instant soup ingredients. Most cooked vegetables can also be pureed and stirred in to thicken soups.

Country Chicken Chowder

1 ½ pounds boneless, skinless chicken breast halves	.7 kg
2 tablespoons butter	30 ml
2 (10 ounce) cans cream of potato soup	2 (280 g)
1 (14 ounce) can chicken broth	396 g
1 (10 ounce) package frozen corn	280 g
1 onion, sliced	
2 ribs celery, sliced	
1 (10 ounce) package frozen peas and carrots, thawed	280 g
½ teaspoon dried thyme leaves	2 ml
½ cup half-and-half cream	120 ml

- Cut chicken into 1-inch (2.5 cm) strips. Brown chicken strips in butter in skillet and transfer to large sprayed slow cooker. Add soup, broth, corn, onion, celery, peas, carrots and thyme to suacepan and heat just enough to mix well. Pour into cooker.

- Cover and cook on LOW for 3 to 4 hours or until vegetables are tender.

- Turn off heat, stir in cream and set aside for about 10 minutes before serving.

Chicken Pasta Soup

1 ½ **pounds boneless, skinless chicken thighs,** **cubed**	**.7 kg**
1 **onion, chopped**	
3 **carrots, sliced**	
½ **cup halved pitted ripe olives**	**120 ml**
1 **teaspoon minced garlic**	**5 ml**
3 **(14 ounce) cans chicken broth**	**3 (396 g)**
1 **(15 ounce) can Italian stewed tomatoes**	**425 g**
1 **teaspoon Italian seasoning**	**5 ml**
½ **cup small shell pasta**	**120 ml**
Parmesan cheese	

- Combine all ingredients, except shell pasta and parmesan cheese in saucepan and heat just enough to mix well. Pour into sprayed slow cooker.

- Cover and cook on LOW for 8 to 9 hours. About 30 minutes before serving, add pasta and stir.

- Increase heat to HIGH and cook another 20 to 30 minutes. Garnish with parmesan cheese.

Tortellini Soup

1 (1 ounce) packet white sauce mix	28 g
3 boneless, skinless chicken breast halves	
1 (14 ounce) can chicken broth	396 g
1 teaspoon minced garlic	5 ml
½ teaspoon dried basil	2 ml
½ teaspoon dried oregano	2 ml
½ teaspoon cayenne pepper	2 ml
1 (8 ounce) package cheese tortellini	227 g
1 ½ cups half-and-half cream	360 ml
1 (10 ounce) package fresh baby spinach	280 g

- Place white sauce mix in sprayed, 5 to 6-quart (5 L) slow cooker. Add 4 cups (1 L) water and stir until mixture is smooth.

- Cut chicken into 1-inch (2.5 cm) pieces. Add chicken, broth, garlic, ½ teaspoon (2 ml) salt, basil, oregano and cayenne pepper to mixture.

- Cover and cook on LOW for 6 to 7 hours or on HIGH for 3 hours.

- Stir in tortellini, cover and cook 1 hour more on HIGH. Stir in cream and fresh spinach and cook just enough for soup to get hot.

Chicken Stew Over Biscuits

2 (1 ounce) packets chicken gravy mix	2 (28 g)
2 cups sliced celery	480 ml
1 (10 ounce) package frozen sliced carrots, thawed	280 g
1 (10 ounce) package frozen green peas, thawed	280 g
1 teaspoon dried basil	5 ml
3 cups cooked, cubed chicken or turkey breasts	710 ml
Buttermilk biscuits	

- Combine gravy mix, 2 cups (480 ml) water, celery, carrots, peas, basil, cubed chicken and ¾ teaspoon (4 ml) each of salt and pepper in slow cooker.

- Cover and cook on LOW for 6 to 7 hours. Serve over baked refrigerated buttermilk biscuits.

   TIP: If you like thick stew, mix 2 tablespoons (30 ml) cornstarch with ¼ cup (60 ml) water and stir into chicken mixture. Cook another 30 minutes to thicken.

A team of scientists at the University of Nebraska confirms what grandmothers have known for centuries – that chicken soup is good for colds. Chicken soup contains several anti-inflammatory ingredients that affect the immune system.

Chicken Stew

4 large boneless, skinless chicken breasts,
   cubed
3 medium potatoes, peeled, cubed
1 (26 ounce) jar meatless spaghetti sauce   737 g
1 (15 ounce) can cut green beans, drained   425 g
1 (15 ounce) can whole kernel corn, drained   425 g
1 tablespoon chicken seasoning   15 ml

- Combine cubed chicken, potatoes, spaghetti sauce, green beans, corn, chicken seasoning and ¾ cup (180 ml) water in 5 to 6-quart (5 L) slow cooker.

- Cover and cook on LOW for 6 to 7 hours.

Chicken-Tortellini Stew

1 (9 ounce) package cheese tortellini   255 g
2 small yellow squash, halved, sliced
1 sweet red bell pepper, seeded, chopped
1 onion, chopped
2 (14 ounce) cans chicken broth   2 (396 g)
1 teaspoon dried rosemary   5 ml
½ teaspoon dried basil   2 ml
2 cups cooked, chopped chicken   480 ml

- Place tortellini, squash, bell pepper and onion in slow cooker. Stir in broth, rosemary, basil and chicken.

- Cover and cook on LOW for 2 to 4 hours or until tortellini and vegetables are tender.

Creamy Dreamy Turkey Soup

1 (8 ounce) carton fresh mushrooms	227 g
2 - 3 cups chopped, cooked turkey breast	480 ml
1 large onion, minced	
6 - 8 baby carrots, diced	
2 (10 ounce) cans cream of chicken soup	2 (280 g)
½ cup chicken broth	120 ml
1 (7 ounce) can green peas, drained	198 g
1 (4 ounce) jar diced pimentos, drained	114 g
½ cup milk	120 ml

- Clean mushrooms, remove stems and make 4 slices of each mushroom. Transfer to sprayed slow cooker. Add turkey, onion, carrots, soup and chicken broth and mix well.

- Cook on LOW for 7 to 8 hours or on HIGH for 3 to 4 hours. Add peas, pimentos and milk and stir well. Cook on LOW for additional 30 minutes or HIGH for 15 minutes.

Turkey-Tortilla Soup

This is a great day-after-Thanksgiving meal.

2 (14 ounce) cans chicken broth	2 (396 g)
2 (15 ounce) cans Mexican stewed tomatoes	2 (425 g)
1 (16 ounce) package frozen succotash, thawed	.5kg
2 teaspoons chili powder	10 ml
1 teaspoon dried cilantro	5 ml
2 cups crushed tortilla chips, divided	480 ml
2 ½ cups chopped, cooked turkey	600 ml

- Combine broth, tomatoes, succotash, chili powder, cilantro, ⅓ cup (80 ml) crushed tortilla chips and turkey or chicken in large slow cooker and stir well. Cover and cook on LOW for 3 to 5 hours. When ready to serve, sprinkle remaining chips over each serving.

Turkey Tortellini Tomato Soup

1 (16 ounce) package turkey sausage	.5 kg
2 (15 ounce) cans Italian stewed tomatoes	2 (425 g)
1 (14 ounce) can chicken broth	396 g
2 (10 ounce) cans French onion soup	2 (280 g)
1 (12 ounce) package coleslaw mix	340 g
1 (9 ounce) package cheese tortellini	255 g

- Brown and crumble turkey sausage in skillet, drain and place in large, sprayed slow cooker. Add tomatoes, chicken broth, onion soup, coleslaw mix and 2 cups (480 ml) water.

- Cover and cook on LOW heat for 5 to 6 hours.

- Turn heat to HIGH and add tortellini. Cover and cook for another 20 minutes.

Turkey-Mushroom Soup

Here's another great way to use leftover chicken or turkey.

2 cups sliced shitake mushrooms	480 ml
2 ribs celery, sliced	
1 small onion, chopped	
2 tablespoons butter	30 ml
1 (15 ounce) can sliced carrots, drained	425 g
2 (14 ounce) cans chicken broth	2 (396 g)
½ cup orzo pasta	120 ml
2 cups cooked, chopped turkey or chicken	480 ml

- Saute mushrooms, celery and onion in butter in skillet. Transfer to slow cooker and add carrots, broth, orzo and turkey. (Do not use smoked turkey.)

- Cover and cook on LOW for 2 to 3 hours or on HIGH for 1 to 2 hours.

    TIP: *Button mushrooms are fine for this recipe too.*

Turkey Veggie Chili

1 pound ground turkey	.5 kg
2 (15 ounce) cans pinto beans with liquid	2 (425 g)
1 (15 ounce) can great northern beans with liquid	425 g
1 (14 ounce) can chicken broth	396 g
2 (15 ounce) cans Mexican stewed tomatoes	2 (425 g)
1 (8 ounce) can whole kernel corn, drained	227 g
1 (16 ounce) package frozen chopped onions and bell peppers, thawed	.5 kg
2 teaspoons minced garlic	10 ml
2 teaspoons ground cumin	10 ml
½ cup elbow macaroni	120 ml

- Cook and brown turkey in skillet with a little oil and place in large slow cooker. Add beans, broth, tomatoes, corn, onions, bell peppers, garlic, cumin and a little salt and stir well.

- Cover and cook on LOW for 4 to 5 hours. Stir in macaroni and continue cooking for about 15 minutes.

- Stir to make sure macaroni does not stick to cooker and cook another 15 minutes or until macaroni is tender.

TIP: If you want to get "fancy," top each serving with dab of sour cream or 1 tablespoon (15 ml) shredded cheddar cheese.

Beef and Barley Soup

1 pound lean ground beef	.5 kg
3 (14 ounce) cans beef broth	3 (396 g)
¾ cup quick-cooking barley	180 ml
1 (16 ounce) package frozen chopped onions	
and bell peppers	.5 kg
3 cups sliced carrots	170 ml
2 cups sliced celery	480 ml
2 teaspoons beef seasoning	10 ml

- Brown ground beef in skillet, drain and transfer to 5-quart (5 L) slow cooker. Add beef broth, barley, onions, bell peppers, carrots, celery and beef seasoning. Cover and cook on LOW for 7 to 8 hours.

Beef Black Bean Soup

1 pound lean ground beef	.5 kg
2 onions, chopped	
2 cups sliced celery	480 ml
2 (14 ounce) cans beef broth	2 (396 g)
1 (15 ounce) can Mexican stewed tomatoes	425 g
2 (15 ounce) cans black beans, rinsed, drained	2 (425 g)

- Brown beef in skillet until no longer pink. Place in sprayed 5 to 6-quart (5 L) slow cooker.

- Add onions, celery, broth, tomatoes, black beans, ¾ cup (180 ml) water and a little salt and pepper.

- Cover and cook on LOW for 6 to 7 hours or on HIGH for 3½ hours.

  TIP: If you like zestier soup, add 1 teaspoon (5 ml) chili powder.

Tasty Cabbage and Beef Soup

1 pound lean ground beef	.5 kg
1 (16 ounce) package coleslaw mix	.5 kg
1 (15 ounce) can cut green beans	425 g
1 (15 ounce) can whole kernel corn	425 g
2 (15 ounce) cans Italian stewed tomatoes	2 (425 g)
2 (14 ounce) cans beef broth	2 (425 g)

- Brown ground beef in skillet, drain fat and place in large slow cooker.

- Add slaw mix, green beans, corn, tomatoes and beef broth and a little salt and pepper. Cover and cook on LOW for 7 to 8 hours. Serve with

Saucy Cabbage Soup

1 pound lean ground beef	.5 kg
1 small head cabbage, chopped	
2 (15 ounce) cans jalapeno pinto beans with	
liquid	2 (425 g)
1 (15 ounce) can tomato sauce	425 g
1 (15 ounce) can Mexican stewed tomatoes	425 g
1 (14 ounce) can beef broth	396 g
2 teaspoons ground cumin	10 ml

- Brown ground beef in skillet, drain and place in sprayed 5 to 6-quart (5 L) slow cooker. Add cabbage, beans, tomato sauce, tomatoes, broth, cumin and 1 cup (240 ml) water and mix well.

- Cover and cook on LOW for 5 to 6 hours or until cabbage is tender.

Chili Soup

3 (15 ounce) cans chili with beans	3 (425 g)
1 (15 ounce) can whole kernel corn	425 g
1 (14 ounce) can beef broth	396 g
2 (15 ounce) cans Mexican stewed tomatoes	2 (425 g)
2 teaspoons ground cumin	10 ml
2 teaspoons chili powder	10 ml

- Combine chili, corn, broth, tomatoes, cumin, chili powder and 1 cup (240 ml) water in 5 to 6-quart (5 L) slow cooker.

- Cover and cook on LOW for 4 to 5 hours. Serve with warm, buttered flour tortillas.

Beef Noodle Soup

1 ½ pounds lean ground beef	.7 kg
1 onion, chopped	
2 (15 ounce) cans mixed vegetables, drained	2 (425 g)
2 (15 ounce) cans Italian stewed tomatoes	2 (425 g)
2 (14 ounce) cans beef broth	2 (396 g)
1 teaspoon dried oregano	5 ml
1 (10 ounce) package medium egg noodles	280 g

- Brown and cook ground beef until no longer pink in skillet and transfer to slow cooker.

- Add onion, mixed vegetables, stewed tomatoes, beef broth and oregano. Cover and cook on LOW for 4 to 5 hours.

- Cook noodles according to package directions. Add noodles to slow cooker and cook for 20 minutes.

Enchilada Soup

1 pound lean ground beef, browned, drained	.5 kg
1 (15 ounce) can Mexican stewed tomatoes	425 g
1 (15 ounce) can pinto beans with liquid	425 g
1 (15 ounce) can whole kernel corn with liquid	425 g
1 onion, chopped	
2 (10 ounce) cans enchilada sauce	2 (280 g)
1 (8 ounce) package shredded 4-cheese blend	227 g

- Combine beef, tomatoes, beans, corn, onion, enchilada sauce and 1 cup (240 ml) water in sprayed 5 to 6-quart (5 L) slow cooker and mix well.

- Cover and cook on LOW for 6 to 8 hours or on HIGH for 3 to 4 hours. Stir in shredded cheese. If desired, top each serving with a few crushed tortilla chips.

Mexican Meatball Soup

3 (14 ounce) cans beef broth	3 (396 g)
1 (16 ounce) jar hot salsa	.5 kg
1 (16 ounce) package frozen corn, thawed	.5 kg
1 (18 ounce) package frozen meatballs, thawed	510 g
1 teaspoon minced garlic	5 ml

- Combine all ingredients in slow cooker and stir well. Cover and cook on LOW for 4 to 7 hours.

Beefy Rice Soup

1 pound lean beef stew meat	.5 kg
1 (14 ounce) can beef broth	396 g
1 (7 ounce) box beef-flavored rice and	
vermicelli mix	198 g
1 (10 ounce) package frozen peas and carrots	280 g
2 ½ cups vegetable juice	600 ml

- Sprinkle stew meat with pepper, brown in non-stick skillet, drain and place in large slow cooker.

- Add broth, rice and vermicelli mix, peas, carrots, vegetable juice and 2 cups (480 ml) water.

- Cover and cook on LOW for 6 to 7 hours.

Meatball Potato Soup

1 (32 ounce) package frozen meatballs	1 kg
2 (15 ounce) cans stewed tomatoes	2 (425 g)
3 large potatoes, peeled, diced	
4 carrots, peeled, sliced	
2 medium onions, chopped	
2 (14 ounce) cans beef broth	2 (396 g)
2 tablespoons cornstarch	30 ml

- Combine meatballs, tomatoes, potatoes, carrots, onions, beef broth, a little salt and pepper and 1 cup (240 ml) water in sprayed 6-quart (6 L) slow cooker.

- Cover and cook on LOW for 5 to 6 hours.

- Turn heat to HIGH. Combine cornstarch with ¼ cup (60 ml) water, pour into cooker and stir to mix well. Cook another 10 or 15 minutes or until slightly thick.

Taco Soup

1 ½ **pounds lean ground beef**	.7 kg
1 **onion, chopped**	
1 **(1 ounce) packet taco seasoning mix**	28 g
1 **(15 ounce) can whole kernel corn with liquid**	425 g
1 **(15 ounce) can pinto beans with liquid**	425 g
1 **(15 ounce) can stewed tomatoes with liquid**	425 g
1 **(14 ounce) can beef broth**	396 g

- Combine beef and onion in large skillet, brown and drain. Transfer to slow cooker.

- Add taco seasoning, corn, beans, tomatoes, 1 cup (240 ml) water and broth and stir well. Cook on LOW for 3 to 4 hours. Serve with tortilla chips.

    TIP: If you want a garnish or something else to put in soup, add chopped chives and a dollop of sour cream.

    TIP: If you don't want to wait 3 to 4 hours, put ingredients in a large soup pot. Boil, reduce heat and simmer for 1 to 2 hours.

Hamburger Soup

2 pounds lean ground beef	1 kg
2 (15 ounce) cans chili without beans	2 (425 g)
1 (16 ounce) package frozen mixed vegetables, thawed	.5 kg
3 (14 ounce) cans beef broth	3 (396 g)
2 (15 ounce) cans stewed tomatoes	2 (425 g)

- Brown ground beef until no longer pink in skillet and place in 6-quart (6 L) slow cooker. Add chili, vegetables, broth, tomatoes, 1 cup (240 ml) water and 1 teaspoon (5 ml) salt and stir well.

- Cover and cook on LOW for 6 to 7 hours.

Taco Soup Olé

2 pounds lean ground beef	1 kg
2 (15 ounce) cans ranch-style beans with liquid	2 (425 g)
1 (15 ounce) can whole kernel corn, drained	425 g
2 (15 ounce) cans stewed tomatoes	2 (425 g)
1 (10 ounce) can tomatoes and green chilies	280 g
1 (1 ounce) package ranch-style dressing mix	28 g
1 (1 ounce) packet taco seasoning mix	28 g

- Brown ground beef in large skillet, drain and transfer to slow cooker. Add remaining ingredients and stir well. Cover and cook on LOW for 8 to 10 hours.

    TIP: If you have some shredded cheddar cheese, it's fun to sprinkle some over each serving.

Camp Stew in Slow Cooker

1 pound lean ground beef	.5 kg
1 onion, chopped	
2 large potatoes, peeled, diced	
1 (15 ounce) can pinto beans	425 g
1 (15 ounce) can cream-style corn	425 g
1 (8 ounce) can whole kernel corn, drained	227 g
2 (12 ounce) cans white chicken meat with liquid	2 (340 g)
2 (15 ounce) cans stewed tomatoes	2 (425 g)
1 cup ketchup	240 ml
2 tablespoons lemon juice	30 ml
1 tablespoon Worcestershire sauce	15 ml
1 teaspoon hot sauce	5 ml

- Brown and cook beef and onion in large skillet over medium heat and stir until beef crumbles and is no longer pink; drain. Layer potatoes, pinto beans, cooked beef, cream-style corn and remaining ingredients in 6-quart (6 L) slow cooker. Cook, covered, on LOW for 8 hours or until potatoes are tender.

Meatball-Veggie Stew

1 (18 ounce) package frozen cooked meatballs, thawed	510 g
1 (16 ounce) package frozen stew vegetables	.5 kg
1 (15 ounce) can stewed tomatoes	425 g
1 (12 ounce) jar beef gravy	340 g
2 teaspoons crushed dried basil	10 ml

- Place meatballs and vegetables in 4 to 5-quart (4 L) slow cooker. Stir stewed tomatoes, gravy, basil, ½ teaspoon (2 ml) pepper and ½ cup (120 ml) water in bowl and mix well. Transfer to slow cooker. Cover and cook on LOW for 6 to 7 hours.

Taco-Chili Soup

2 pounds very lean stew meat	1 kg
2 (15 ounce) cans Mexican stewed tomatoes	2 (425 g)
1 (1 ounce) packet taco seasoning mix	28 g
2 (15 ounce) cans pinto beans with liquid	2 (425 g)
1 (15 ounce) can whole kernel corn with liquid	425 g

- Cut large pieces of stew meat in half and brown in large skillet.

- Combine stew meat, tomatoes, taco seasoning, beans, corn and ¾ cup (180 ml) water in 4 or 5-quart (4 L) slow cooker.

- Cover and cook on LOW for 5 to 7 hours.

  TIP: *If you are not into "spicy," use the original stewed tomatoes instead of Mexican stewed tomatoes.*

Hearty Meatball Stew

1 (32 ounce) package frozen meatballs, thawed	1 kg
2 (15 ounce) cans Italian stewed tomatoes	2 (425 g)
2 (14 ounce) cans beef broth	2 (396 g)
2 (15 ounce) cans new potatoes, drained	2 (425 g)
1 (16 ounce) package baby carrots	.5 kg
1 tablespoon beef seasoning	15 ml

- Place meatballs, stewed tomatoes, beef broth, potatoes, carrots and beef seasoning in 6-quart (6 L) slow cooker.

- Cover and cook on LOW for 6 to 7 hours. Serve with corn muffins.

Comfort Stew

1 ½ pounds premium stew meat	.7 kg
2 (10 ounce) cans French onion soup	2 (280 g)
1 (10 ounce) can cream of onion soup	280 g
1 (10 ounce) can cream of celery soup	280 g
1 (16 ounce) package frozen stew vegetables, thawed	.5 kg

- Place stew meat in sprayed slow cooker. Combine all soups and mix well. Spread evenly over meat, but do not stir.

- Turn slow cooker to HIGH and cook just long enough for ingredients to get hot, about 15 minutes.

- Change heat setting to LOW, cover and cook for 7 hours. Add vegetables and cook 1 more hour.

South-of-the-Border Beef Stew

1 ½ - 2 pounds boneless, beef chuck roast	.7 kg
1 green bell pepper	
2 onions, coarsely chopped	
2 (15 ounce) cans pinto beans with liquid	2 (425 g)
½ cup uncooked rice	120 ml
1 (14 ounce) can beef broth	396 g
2 (15 ounce) cans Mexican stewed tomatoes	2 (425 g)
1 cup mild or medium green salsa	240 ml
2 teaspoons ground cumin	10 ml

- Trim beef and cut into 1-inch (2.5 cm) cubes. Brown beef in large skillet and transfer to large sprayed slow cooker.

- Cut bell pepper into ½-inch (1.2 cm) slices. Add remaining ingredients with a little salt and 1 ½ cups (360 ml) water.

- Cover and cook on LOW for 7 to 8 hours. Serve with warm flour tortillas.

Gringo Stew Pot

1 ½ - 2 pounds lean beef stew meat	.7 kg
2 (15 ounce) cans pinto beans with liquid	2 (425 g)
1 onion, chopped	
3 carrots, sliced	
2 medium potatoes, peeled, cubed	
1 (1 ounce) packet taco seasoning mix	28 g
2 (15 ounce) cans Mexican stewed tomatoes	2 (425 g)

- Brown stew meat in non-stick skillet. Combine meat, pinto beans, onion, carrots, potatoes, taco seasoning and 2 cups (480 ml) water in large slow cooker.

- Cover and cook on LOW for 6 to 7 hours. Add stewed tomatoes and cook 1 more hour.

  TIP: This is great served with warmed, buttered flour tortillas.

A Different Stew

2 pounds premium-cut stew meat	1 kg
1 (16 ounce) package frozen Oriental stir-fry vegetables, thawed	.5 kg
1 (10 ounce) can beefy mushroom soup	280 g
1 (10 ounce) can beef broth	280 g
⅔ cup bottled sweet-and-sour sauce	160 ml
1 tablespoon beef seasoning	15 ml

- Sprinkle stew meat with ½ teaspoon (2 ml) pepper, brown in skillet and transfer to slow cooker.

- Combine vegetables, soup, broth, sweet-and-sour sauce, beef seasoning and 1 cup (240 ml) water in bowl. Pour over stew meat and stir well. Cover and cook on LOW for 7 to 8 hours.

Roast and Vegetable Stew

3 cups roast beef, cooked, cubed	710 ml
2 (15 ounce) cans stewed tomatoes	2 (425 g)
1 (16 ounce) package frozen mixed vegetables, thawed	.5 kg
2 (14 ounce) cans beef broth	2 (396 g)

- Combine all ingredients in 6-quart (6 L) slow cooker with salt and pepper to taste. Cover and cook on LOW for 5 to 7 hours.

TIP: If you want some crunchy vegetables in your soup, add 1 cup (240 ml) cauliflower florets and 1 cup (240 ml) broccoli florets about 1 hour before serving.

Hungarian Stew

2 pounds boneless short ribs	1 kg
1 cup pearl barley	240 ml
1 small onion, chopped	
1 green bell pepper, seeded, chopped	
1 teaspoon prepared minced garlic	5 ml
2 (15 ounce) cans kidney beans, drained	2 (425 g)
2 (14 ounce) cans beef broth	2 (396 g)
1 tablespoon paprika	15 ml

- Combine all ingredients plus 1 cup (240 ml) water in slow cooker.

- Cover and cook on LOW for 8 to 9 hours or on HIGH for 4½ to 5 hours.

Easy Chili

4 pounds lean ground beef	1.8 kg
2 (10 ounce) packages hot chili mix	2 (280 g)
1 (6 ounce) can tomato sauce	168 g
2 (15 ounce) cans stewed tomatoes with liquid	2 (425 g)
2½ teaspoons ground cumin	12 ml

- Break ground beef into pieces, brown in large skillet and drain. Use slotted spoon to drain fat and place beef in 5 to 6-quart (5 L) slow cooker.

- Add chili mix, tomato sauce, stewed tomatoes, cumin, 1 teaspoon (5 ml) salt and 1 cup (240 ml) water.

- Cover and cook on LOW setting for 4 to 5 hours.

  TIP: If you think chili has to have beans, add 2 (15 ounce/425 g) cans ranch-style beans.

Chili Tonight

2 pounds lean beef chili meat	1 kg
1 large onion, finely chopped	
1 (10 ounce) can chopped tomatoes and green chilies	280 g
2½ cups tomato juice	600 ml
2 tablespoons chili powder	30 ml
1 tablespoon ground cumin	15 ml
1 tablespoon minced garlic	15 ml

- Combine chili meat, onion, tomatoes and green chilies, tomato juice, chili powder, cumin, garlic and 1 cup (240 ml) water in large slow cooker and mix well.

- Cover and cook on LOW for 7 to 8 hours.

Chunky Chili

2 pounds premium-cut stew meat	1 kg
1 onion, chopped	
2 (15 ounce) cans diced tomatoes	2 (425 g)
2 (15 ounce) cans pinto beans with liquid	2 (425 g)
1 ½ tablespoons chili powder	.7 kg
2 teaspoons ground cumin	10 ml
1 teaspoon ground oregano	5 ml
Shredded cheddar cheese	

- If stew meat is in fairly large chunks, cut each chunk in half. Brown in large skillet and transfer to large slow cooker.

- Add onion, tomatoes, beans, seasonings and salt to taste. Cover and cook on LOW for 6 to 7 hours.

- Sprinkle shredded cheddar cheese over each serving.

Spicy Black Bean Soup

1 pound hot pork sausage	.5 kg
1 onion, chopped	
2 (14 ounce) cans chicken broth	2 (396 g)
2 (15 ounce) cans Mexican stewed tomatoes	2 (425 g)
1 green bell pepper, seeded, chopped	
2 (15 ounce) cans black beans, rinsed, drained	2 (425 g)

- Break up sausage and brown with onion in large skillet. Drain fat and transfer to large slow cooker.

- Add chicken broth, stewed tomatoes, bell pepper, black beans and 1 cup (240 ml) water. Cover and cook on LOW for 3 to 4 hours.

Black Bean-Chile Soup

2 (14 ounce) cans chicken broth	2 (396 g)
3 (15 ounce) cans black beans, rinsed, drained	3 (425 g)
2 (10 ounce) cans tomatoes and green chilies	2 (280 g)
1 onion, chopped	
1 teaspoon ground cumin	5 ml
½ teaspoon dried thyme	2 ml
½ teaspoon dried oregano	2 ml
2 - 3 cups finely diced, ham	480 ml
1 tablespoon minced garlic	15 ml

- Combine chicken broth and black beans in slow cooker and cook on HIGH just long enough for ingredients to get hot. With potato masher, mash about half of beans in cooker.

- Reduce heat to LOW and add tomatoes and green chilies, onion, spices, ham and ¾ cup (180 ml) water.

- Cover and cook for 5 to 6 hours.

Cajun Bean Soup

1 (20 ounce) package Cajun-flavored, 16-bean soup mix with flavor packet	567 g
2 cups finely chopped, cooked ham	480 ml
1 onion, chopped	
2 (15 ounce) cans stewed tomatoes	2 (425 g)

- Soak beans overnight in large slow cooker. After soaking, drain water and cover with 2 inches (5 cm) water over beans. Cover and cook on LOW for 5 to 6 hours or until beans are tender.

- Add ham, onion, stewed tomatoes and flavor packet in bean soup mix. Cook on HIGH for 30 to 45 minutes. Serve with cornbread.

Southern Soup

1 ½ cups dry black-eyed peas	360 ml
2 - 3 cups cooked, cubed ham	480 ml
1 (15 ounce) can whole kernel corn, drained	425 g
1 (10 ounce) package frozen cut okra, thawed	280 g
1 onion, chopped	
1 large potato, peeled, cubed	
2 teaspoons Cajun seasoning	10 ml
1 (14 ounce) can chicken broth	396 g
2 (15 ounce) cans Mexican stewed tomatoes	2 (425 g)

- Rinse peas and drain. Combine peas and 5 cups (1.3 L) water in large saucepan. Boil, reduce heat and simmer about 10 minutes. Drain peas and pour into 5 or 6-quart (5 L) slow cooker.

- Pour ham, corn, okra, onion, potato, seasoning, broth and 2 cups (480 ml) water into slow cooker, cover and cook on LOW for 6 to 8 hours.

- Add stewed tomatoes and continue cooking for 1 more hour.

Black Eyed Pea Soup

5 slices thick-cut bacon, diced
1 onion, chopped
1 green bell pepper, seeded, chopped
3 ribs celery, sliced
3 (15 ounce) cans jalapeno black-eyed peas
   with liquid   3 (425 g)
2 (15 ounce) cans stewed tomatoes with liquid   2 (425 g)
1 teaspoon chicken seasoning   5 ml

- Cook bacon pieces until crisp in skillet, drain on paper towel and drop in slow cooker.

- With bacon drippings in skillet, saute onion and bell pepper, but do not brown.

- Transfer onions and bell pepper to slow cooker. Add celery, black-eyed peas, stewed tomatoes, 1 ½ cups (360 ml) water, 1 teaspoon (5 ml) salt and chicken seasoning.

- Cover and cook on LOW for 3 to 4 hours.

Navy Bean-Bacon Soup

8 slices thick-cut bacon, divided
1 carrot, halved lengthwise, sliced
3 (15 ounce) cans navy beans with liquid   3 (425 g)
3 ribs celery, chopped
1 onion, chopped
2 (15 ounce) cans chicken broth   2 (425 g)
1 teaspoon Italian herb seasoning   5 ml
1 (10 ounce) can cream of chicken soup   280 g

- Cook bacon in skillet, drain and crumble. Combine most
  of crumbled bacon, carrot, beans, celery, onion, broth,
  seasoning and 1 cup (240 ml) water in 5 to 6-quart (5 L)
  slow cooker. Cover and cook on LOW for 5 to 6 hours.

- Ladle 2 cups (480 ml) soup mixture into blender and
  process until smooth. Return to cooker, add soup and stir
  to mix.

- Cook on HIGH for another 10 to 15 minutes. Sprinkle
  remaining bacon crumbles on top of soup before serving.

*You can give canned broth a little extra flavor by
simmering reserved chicken or meat bones in the broth for
15 minutes. Strain the liquid and use it for your soup.*

Ham and Bean Soup

3 cups cooked, cubed ham	710 ml
1 onion, finely chopped	
2 ribs celery, chopped	
2 teaspoons minced garlic	10 ml
2 (14 ounce) cans chicken broth	2 (396 g)
2 (15 ounce) cans pork and beans with liquid	2 (425 g)
⅓ cup pasta shells	80 ml

- Combine onion, celery, garlic, chicken broth, beans, ham and 1 cup (240 ml) water in 5 or 6-quart (5 L) slow cooker.

- Cover and cook on LOW for 4 to 5 hours.

- Turn cooker to HIGH heat, add pasta and cook another 35 to 45 minutes or until pasta is tender.

    TIP: If you have time to fry some bacon, it's great crumbled on top of soup as garnish.

Slow-Cook Navy Bean Soup

Better than Grandma's!

1 ½ cups dried navy beans	360 ml
1 bell pepper, seeded, chopped	
1 carrot, finely chopped	
2 celery ribs, finely chopped	
1 small onion, finely chopped	
1 (1 pound) ham hock	.5 kg

- Soak beans for 8 to 12 hours and drain. Place all ingredients in 2-quart (2 L) slow cooker, add 5 cups (1.3 L) water and ½ teaspoon (2 ml) salt and pepper to taste. Cook for 8 to 10 hours on LOW setting.

- Remove ham hock and discard skin, fat and bone. Cut meat in small pieces and place in soup. Beans can be mashed, if desired.

Need to thicken your soup? Adding a little pasta or mashed potato flakes is a great way to add bulk to your soup.

Pork and Hominy Soup

2 pounds pork shoulder, cubed	1 kg
1 onion, chopped	
2 ribs celery, sliced	
2 (15 ounce) cans yellow hominy with liquid	2 (425 g)
2 (15 ounce) cans stewed tomatoes	2 (425 g)
2 (14 ounce) cans chicken broth	2 (396 g)
1 tablespoon ground cumin	15 ml
Tortillas	
Shredded cheese	
Green onions, chopped	

- Sprinkle pork cubes with salt and pepper and brown in skillet. Place in 5 to 6-quart (5 L) slow cooker.

- Combine onion, celery, hominy, stewed tomatoes, broth, ground cumin and 1 cup (240 ml) water and pour over pork. Cover and cook on HIGH for 6 to 7 hours.

- Serve with warmed, buttered tortillas and top each bowl of soup with some shredded cheese and green onions.

Winter Minestrone

1 pound uncooked Italian sausage links, sliced	.5 kg
2 medium potatoes, peeled, cubed	
2 medium fennel bulbs, trimmed, chopped	
2 ½ cups peeled, chopped, butternut or	
acorn squash	600 ml
1 onion, chopped	
1 (15 ounce) can kidney beans, rinsed, drained	425 g
2 teaspoons prepared minced garlic	10 ml
1 teaspoon Italian seasoning	5 ml
2 (14 ounce) cans chicken broth	2 (396 g)
1 cup dry white wine	240 ml
1 (10 ounce) package fresh spinach,	
stems removed	280 g

- Cook sausage until brown in skillet and drain.

- Combine potatoes, fennel, squash, onion, beans, garlic and Italian seasoning in large slow cooker.

- Top with sausage and pour chicken broth and wine over all.

- Cover and cook on LOW for 7 to 9 hours.

- Stir in spinach, cover and cook for 10 more minutes.

Tater Talk Soup

5 medium potatoes, peeled, cubed	
2 cups cooked, cubed ham	480 ml
1 cup chopped, fresh broccoli florets	240 ml
1 (10 ounce) can cheddar cheese soup	280 g
1 (10 ounce) can fiesta nacho cheese soup	280 g
1 (14 ounce) can chicken broth	396 g
2 ½ soups can milk	

• Place potatoes, ham and broccoli in sprayed slow cooker.

• Combine soups, broth and milk in saucepan and heat just
  enough to mix until smooth. Pour ingredients in slow
  cooker. Cover and cook on LOW for 7 to 8 hours.

Potato Soup

3 large potatoes, peeled, cubed	
¼ cup (½ stick) butter, sliced	60 ml
1 (14 ounce) can chicken broth	396 g
1 onion, finely chopped	
2 cups milk	480 ml
2 cups cooked, cubed ham	480 ml
1 (8 ounce) package cubed Velveeta® cheese	227 g
1 teaspoon dried parsley	5 ml
1 (8 ounce) carton whipping cream	227 g

• Place potatoes, butter, broth, onion, milk and 2 cups (480
  ml) water in sprayed 6-cup (1.5 L) slow cooker. Cook on
  HIGH for 30 minutes, reduce heat to LOW, cover and cook 6
  to 7 hours.

• Stir in ham, cheese, parsley and a little salt and pepper and
  cook on HIGH for 20 minutes or until cheese melts. Stir in
  whipping cream and serve hot.

Spicy Sausage Soup

1 pound mild bulk sausage	.5 kg
1 pound hot bulk sausage	.5 kg
2 (15 ounce) cans Mexican stewed tomatoes	2 (425 g)
3 cups chopped celery	710 ml
1 (8 ounce) can sliced carrots, drained	227g
1 (15 ounce) can cut green beans, drained	425 g
1 (14 ounce) can chicken broth	396 g

- Combine mild and hot sausage, shape into small balls and place in non-stick skillet. Brown thoroughly, drain and place in large slow cooker.

- Add remaining ingredients with 1 teaspoon (5 ml) salt and 1 cup (240 ml) water to slow cooker and stir gently so meatballs will not break-up. Cover and cook on LOW for 6 to 7 hours.

Potato Leek Soup

1 (1 ounce) packet white sauce mix	28 g
1 (28 ounce) package frozen hash brown potatoes with onions and peppers, thawed	794 g
3 medium leeks, sliced	
3 cups cooked, cubed ham	710 ml
1 (12 ounce) can evaporated milk	340 g
1 (8 ounce) carton sour cream	227 g

- Combine 3 cups (710 ml) water and white sauce in 4 to 5-quart (4 L) slow cooker and stir until smooth.

- Add potatoes, leeks, ham and evaporated milk. Cover and cook on LOW for 7 to 9 hours or on HIGH for 3 to 4 hours.

- When ready to serve, turn heat to HIGH. Remove about 2 cups (480 ml) hot soup and pour into separate bowl.

- Stir in sour cream and return to cooker. Cover and continue cooking for 15 minutes or until mixture is thoroughly hot.

Sausage Pizza Soup

1 (16 ounce) package Italian link sausage, sliced	.5 kg
1 onion, chopped	
2 (4 ounce) cans sliced mushrooms	2 (114 g)
1 green bell pepper, seeded, julienned	
1 (15 ounce) can Italian stewed tomatoes	425 g
1 (14 ounce) can beef broth	396 g
1 (8 ounce) can pizza sauce	227 g

- Combine all ingredients in slow cooker and stir well. Cover and cook on LOW for 4 to 5 hours.

Beans N' Sausage Soup

1 pound hot Italian sausage	.5 kg
1 onion, chopped	
1 (15 ounce) can Italian stewed tomatoes	425 g
2 (5 ounce) cans black beans, rinsed, drained	2 (143 g)
2 (15 ounce) cans navy beans with liquid	2 (425 g)
2 (14 ounce) cans beef broth	2 (396 g)
1 teaspoon minced garlic	5 ml
1 teaspoon dried basil	5 ml

- Cut sausage into ½-inch (1.2 cm) pieces. Brown sausage and onion in skillet, drain and transfer to 5 to 6-quart (5 L) slow cooker.

- Stir in tomatoes, black beans, navy beans, broth, garlic and basil and mix well. Cover and cook on LOW for 5 to 7 hours.

Pork Vegetable Stew

1 (1 pound) pork tenderloin	.5 kg
1 onion, coarsely chopped	
1 sweet red bell pepper, seeded, julienned	
1 (16 ounce) package frozen stew vegetables, thawed	.5 kg
2 tablespoons flour	30 ml
½ teaspoon dried rosemary leaves	2 ml
½ teaspoon oregano leaves	2 ml
1 (14 ounce) can chicken broth	396 g
1 (6 ounce) box long grain-wild rice	168 g

- Cut tenderloin into 1-inch (2.5 cm) cubes and brown in non-stick skillet. Place in large sprayed slow cooker; add onion, bell pepper and mixed vegetables.

- Stir flour, rosemary and oregano into ½ cup (120 ml) water and mix well. Pour seasoning mixture and broth over vegetables.

- Cover and cook on LOW for 5 to 6 hours. When ready to serve, cook rice according to package directions. Serve pork and vegetables over rice.

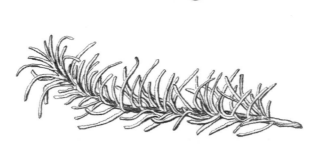

Italian Vegetable Stew

2 pounds Italian sausage	1 kg
2 (16 ounce) packages frozen mixed vegetables	2 (.5 kg)
2 (15 ounce) cans Italian stewed tomatoes	2 (425 g)
1 (14 ounce) can beef broth	1 (396 g)
1 teaspoon Italian seasoning	5 ml
½ cup pasta shells	120 ml

- Brown sausage in skillet, cook about 5 minutes and drain.

- Combine sausage, vegetables, stewed tomatoes, broth and Italian seasoning in 5 to 6-quart (5 L) slow cooker and mix well.

- Cover and cook on LOW for 3 to 5 hours. About 30 minutes before serving, cook shells with stew in slow cooker until they are tender.

Ham and Cabbage Stew

2 (15 ounce) cans Italian stewed tomatoes	2 (425 g)
3 cups shredded cabbage	710 ml
1 onion, chopped	
1 sweet red bell pepper, seeded, chopped	
2 tablespoons butter	30 ml
1 (14 ounce) can chicken broth	396 g
3 cups cooked, diced ham	710 ml

- Combine all ingredients plus ¾ teaspoon (4 ml) each of salt and pepper and 1 cup (240 ml) water in large slow cooker and mix well.

- Cover and cook on LOW for 5 to 7 hours.

Southern Ham Stew

This is a great meal and it screams for cornbread.

2 cups dried black-eyed peas	480 ml
3 cups cubed, cooked ham	710 ml
1 large onion, chopped	
2 cups sliced celery	480 ml
1 (15 ounce) can yellow hominy, drained	425
2 (15 ounce) cans stewed tomatoes	2 (425 g)
1 (14 ounce) can chicken broth	396 g
2 tablespoons cornstarch	30 ml

- Rinse and drain dried black-eyed peas in saucepan. Cover peas with water, boil and drain again. Place peas in large slow cooker and add 5 cups (1.3 L) water, ham, onion, celery, hominy, tomatoes and broth.

- Cover and cook on LOW for 7 to 9 hours. Mix cornstarch with ⅓ cup (80 ml) water, turn cooker to HIGH, pour in cornstarch mixture and stir well.

- Cook just about 10 minutes or until stew thickens. Add good amount of salt and pepper and stir well before serving.

TIP: If you would like a little spice in the stew, substitute stewed tomatoes for Mexican stewed tomatoes.

Vegetable Chili

2 (15 ounce) cans navy beans with liquid	2 (425 g)
1 (15 ounce) can pinto beans with liquid	425 g
2 (15 ounce) cans Mexican stewed tomatoes	2 (425 g)
1 (15 ounce) can whole kernel corn	425 g
1 onion, chopped	
3 ribs celery, sliced	
1 tablespoon chili powder	15 ml
2 teaspoons dried oregano leaves	10 ml

- Combine navy beans, pinto beans, tomatoes, corn, onion, celery, chili powder, oregano, 1 teaspoon (5 ml) salt and 1 ½ cups (360 ml) water in 5 to 6-quart (5 L) slow cooker.

- Cover and cook on LOW for 4 to 6 hours.

Serious Bean Stew

1 (16 ounce) package smoked sausage links	.5 kg
1 (28 ounce) can baked beans with liquid	794 g
1 (15 ounce) can great northern beans with liquid	425 g
1 (15 ounce) can pinto beans with liquid	425 g
1 (10 ounce) can French onion soup	280 g
1 onion, chopped	
1 teaspoon Cajun seasoning	5 ml
2 (15 ounce) cans stewed tomatoes	2 (425 g)

- Peel skin from sausage links and slice. Place in 6-quart (6 L) slow cooker, add remaining ingredients and stir to mix.

- Cover and cook on LOW for 3 to 4 hours. Serve with corn muffins.

Ham-Vegetable Chowder

*When you bake a big ham, always make sure you have plenty
leftover for this recipe.*

1 medium potato, peeled	
2 (10 ounce) cans cream of celery soup	2 (280 g)
1 (14 ounce) can chicken broth	396 g
3 cups cooked, finely diced ham	710 ml
1 (15 ounce) can whole kernel corn	425 g
2 carrots, sliced	
1 onion, coarsely chopped	
1 teaspoon dried basil	5 ml
1 (10 ounce) package frozen broccoli florets	280 g

- Cut potato into 1-inch (2.5 cm) pieces.
  Combine all ingredients except broccoli
  florets with 1 teaspoon (5 ml) each of
  salt and pepper in large slow cooker.

- Cover and cook on LOW for 5 to 6 hours.
  Add broccoli to cooker and cook for 1 more hour.

Split-Pea and Ham Chowder

1 medium potato, peeled	
3 cups cooked, cubed ham	710 ml
1 (16 ounce) package split peas, rinsed	.5 kg
1 (11 ounce) can whole kernel corn with red	
and green peppers	312 g
1 (14 ounce) can chicken broth	396 g
2 carrots, sliced	
2 ribs celery, diagonally sliced	
1 tablespoon dried onion flakes	15 ml
1 teaspoon dried marjoram leaves	5 ml

- Cut potato into small cubes and add to sprayed slow cooker.

- Combine all ingredients plus 3 cups (710 ml) water and 1 teaspoon (5 ml) salt in slow cooker.

- Cover and cook on LOW for 6 to 8 hours.

Herbs will have a more intense flavor if they are added when the soup is almost ready to serve.

Oyster Chowder

1 red bell pepper, seeded, chopped	
1 onion, chopped	
1 (14 ounce) can chicken broth	425 g
1 medium potato peeled, cubed	
1 fresh jalapeno pepper, finely chopped	
1 (8 ounce) carton shucked fresh oysters with liquor	227 g
1 (10 ounce) package frozen whole kernel corn, thawed	280 g
1 teaspoon dried oregano	5 ml
½ cup whipping cream	120 ml

• Combine all ingredients except cream in slow cooker. Cover and cook on LOW for 3 to 4 hours. When ready to serve, stir in cream.

Crab Chowder

2 small zucchini, thinly sliced	
1 sweet red bell pepper, seeded, julienned	
2 ribs celery, diagonally sliced	
1 medium potato, peeled, cubed	
2 tablespoons (¼ stick) butter, melted	30 ml
1 (10 ounce) can chicken broth	280 g
2 tablespoons cornstarch	30 ml
3 cups milk	710 ml
2 (6 ounce) cans crabmeat, drained, flaked	2 (168 g)
1 (3 ounce) package cream cheese, cubed	84 g

• Place zucchini, bell pepper, celery, potato, butter, broth and 1 teaspoon (5 ml) salt in sprayed slow cooker. Stir cornstarch into milk, stir and pour into slow cooker. Cover and cook on LOW for 3 to 4 hours. Turn heat to HIGH, add crabmeat and cream cheese and stir until cream cheese melts.

Shrimp and Chicken Jambalaya

4 boneless, skinless chicken breast halves, cubed	
1 (28 ounce) can diced tomatoes	794 g
1 onion, chopped	
1 green bell pepper, chopped	
1 (14 ounce) can chicken broth	396 g
½ cup dry white wine	120 ml
2 teaspoons dried oregano	10 ml
2 teaspoons Cajun seasoning	10 ml
½ teaspoon cayenne pepper	2 ml
1 pound cooked, peeled, veined shrimp	.5 kg
2 cups cooked white rice	480 ml

- Place all ingredients except shrimp and rice in slow cooker and stir. Cover and cook on LOW for 6 to 8 hours.

- Turn heat to HIGH, stir in shrimp and rice and cook another 15 to 20 minutes.

Wine is a great flavor addition to soups and stews. When using wine or alcohol in soup, use less salt because the wine tends to intensify saltiness. Wine should be added at a ratio of no more than ¼ cup wine to 1 quart soup.

Beans and Barley Soup

2 (15 ounce) cans pinto beans with liquid	2 (420 g)
3 (14 ounce) cans chicken broth	3 (396 g)
½ cup quick-cooking barley	120 ml
1 (15 ounce) can Italian stewed tomatoes	425 g

- Combine beans, broth, barley, stewed tomatoes and ½ teaspoon (2 ml) pepper in 6-quart (6 L) slow cooker and stir well.

- Cover and cook on LOW for 4 to 5 hours.

Italian Bean Soup

2 (15 ounce) cans great northern beans with liquid	2 (425 g)
2 (15) ounce) cans pinto beans with liquid	2 (425 g)
1 large onion, chopped	
1 tablespoon instant beef bouillon	15 ml
1 tablespoon minced garlic	15 ml
2 teaspoons Italian seasoning	10 ml
2 (15 ounce) cans Italian stewed tomatoes	2 (425 g)
1 (15 ounce) can cut green beans, drained	425 g

- Combine both cans of beans, onion, beef bouillon, garlic, Italian seasoning and 2 cups (480 ml) water in large slow cooker.

- Cover and cook on LOW for 6 to 8 hours. Turn heat to HIGH, add stewed tomatoes and green beans and stir well.

- Continue cooking for another 30 minutes or until green beans are tender.

  TIP: Serve with crispy Italian toast.

Delicious Broccoli Cheese Soup

1 (16 ounce) package frozen chopped broccoli, thawed	.5 kg
1 (12 ounce) package cubed Velveeta® cheese	340 g
1 (1 ounce) packet white sauce mix	28 g
1 (1 ounce) packet dry vegetable soup mix	28 g
1 (12 ounce) can evaporated milk	340 g
1 (14 ounce) can chicken broth	396 g

- Combine all ingredients plus 2 cups (480 ml) water in large, sprayed slow cooker and stir well.

- Cover and cook on LOW for 6 to 7 hours or on HIGH for 3 ½ to 4 hours. Stir 1 hour before serving time.

French Onion Soup

5 - 6 sweet onions, thinly sliced	
1 clove garlic, minced	
2 tablespoons (¼ stick) butter	30 ml
2 (14 ounce) cans beef broth	2 (396 g)
2 teaspoons Worcestershire sauce	10 ml
6 - 8 (1-inch) slices French bread	6 - 8 (2.5 cm)
8 slices Swiss cheese	

- Cook onions and garlic on low heat (do not brown) in hot butter in large skillet for about 20 minutes and stir several times. Transfer onion mixture to 4 to 5-quart (4 L) slow cooker. Add beef broth, Worcestershire and 1 cup (240 ml) water.

- Cover and cook on LOW for 5 to 8 hours or on HIGH for 2 ½ to 4 hours.

- Before serving soup, toast bread slices with cheese slice on top. Broil for 3 to 4 minutes or until cheese is light brown and bubbles. Ladle soup into bowls and top with toast.

Cheesy Potato Soup

6 medium potatoes, peeled, cubed
1 onion, very finely chopped
2 (14 ounce) cans chicken broth   2 (396 g)
1 (8 ounce) package shredded American cheese 227 g
1 cup half-and-half cream   240 ml

- Combine potatoes, onion, chicken broth and ½ teaspoon (2 ml) pepper in slow cooker.

- Cover and cook on LOW for 8 to 10 hours. With potato masher, mash potatoes in slow cooker.

- About 1 hour before serving, stir in cheese and cream and cook 1 more hour.

Vegetable-Lentil Soup

2 (19 ounce) cans lentil home-style soup   2 (538 g)
1 (15 ounce) can stewed tomatoes   425 g
1 (14 ounce) can chicken broth   396 g
1 onion, chopped
1 green bell pepper, chopped
3 ribs celery, sliced
1 carrot, halved, sliced
2 teaspoons minced garlic   10 ml
1 teaspoon dried marjoram leaves   5 ml

- Combine all ingredients in slow cooker and stir well.

- Cover and cook on LOW for 5 to 6 hours.

Pinto Bean-Vegetable Soup

4 (15 ounce) cans pinto beans with liquid	4 (425 g)
1 (16 ounce) package frozen chopped	
onions and peppers	.5 kg
2 cups chopped celery	480 ml
2 (14 ounce) cans chicken broth	2 (396 g)
1 teaspoon Cajun seasoning	5 ml

- Place all ingredients plus 1 cup (240 ml) water in 5-quart (5 L) slow cooker and stir well. Cover and cook on LOW 5 to 6 hours.

TIP: If you want to give this soup a little "kick," sprinkle a little cayenne or several drops of hot sauce. They will remember you that way.

Creamy Vegetable Soup

3 (14 ounce) cans chicken broth	3 (396 g)
¼ cup (½ stick) butter, melted	60 ml
1 (16 ounce) package frozen mixed vegetables	.5 kg
1 onion, chopped	
3 ribs celery, sliced	
1 teaspoon ground cumin	5 ml
3 zucchini, coarsely chopped	
2 cups chopped, fresh broccoli	480 ml
1 cup half-and-half cream	240 ml

- Combine broth, butter, mixed vegetables, onion, celery, cumin, 1 teaspoon (5 ml) each of salt and pepper in large slow cooker and stir well.

- Cover and cook on LOW for 6 to 7 hours or on HIGH for 3 to 4 hours. Stir in zucchini and broccoli. Cook another 30 minutes to 1 hour or until broccoli is tender-crisp.

- Turn off heat and stir in cream. Let stand for 10 minutes before serving.

Pizza Soup

3 (10 ounce) cans tomato-bisque soup	3 (280 g)
1 (10 ounce) can French onion soup	280 g
2 teaspoons Italian seasoning	10 ml
¾ cup uncooked tiny pasta shells	180 ml
1 ½ cups shredded mozzarella cheese	360 ml

- Place both soups, Italian seasoning and 1 ½ soup cans water in 4 to 6-quart (4 L) slow cooker. Cook 1 hour on HIGH or until mixture is hot. Add pasta shells and cook for 1 ½ to 2 hours or until pasta cooks. Stir several times to keep pasta from sticking to bottom of slow cooker.

- Turn heat off, add mozzarella cheese and stir until cheese melts.

TIP: *If you want a special way to serve this soup, sprinkle some french-fried onions over top of each serving.*

Soup With A Zip

2 (15 ounce) cans Mexican stewed tomatoes	2 (425 g)
2 (14 ounce) cans chicken broth	2 (396 g)
2 (10 ounce) cans chicken noodle soup	2 (280 g)
1 (15 ounce) can shoe-peg corn, drained	425 g
1 (15 ounce) can cut green beans, drained	425 g
Shredded pepper-Jack cheese	

- Place all ingredients except cheese in 4 to 5-quart (4 L) slow cooker and mix well.

- Cover and cook on LOW for 2 to 3 hours. When ready to serve, sprinkle shredded cheese over each bowl of soup.

Minestrone Soup

2 (15 ounce) cans Italian stewed tomatoes	2 (425 g)
2 (16 ounce) packages frozen vegetables	
and pasta-seasoned sauce	2 (.5 kg)
3 (14 ounce) cans beef broth	3 (396 g)
2 ribs celery, chopped	
2 potatoes, peeled, cubed	
1 teaspoon Italian herb seasoning	5 ml
2 (15 ounce) cans kidney beans, rinsed, drained	2 (425 g)
2 teaspoons minced garlic	10 ml

- Combine all ingredients with 1 cup (240 ml) water in large sprayed slow cooker and mix well.

- Cover and cook on LOW for 4 to 6 hours.

Pasta-Veggie Soup

2 yellow squash, chopped	
2 zucchini, sliced	
1 (10 ounce) package frozen corn, thawed	280 g
1 sweet red bell pepper, seeded, chopped	
1 (15 ounce) can stewed tomatoes	425 g
1 teaspoon Italian seasoning	5 ml
2 teaspoons dried oregano	10 ml
2 (14 ounce) cans beef broth	2 (396 g)
¾ cup uncooked small shell pasta	180 ml

- Combine squash, zucchini, corn, bell pepper, tomatoes, Italian seasoning, oregano, beef broth and 2 cups (480 ml) water in 6-quart (6 L) slow cooker. Cover and cook on LOW for 6 to 7 hours.

- Add pasta shells and cook additional 30 to 45 minutes or until pasta is tender.

C

S

Teaspoon
¼ teaspoon.............................. 1 ml
½ teaspoon.............................. 2 ml
⅓ teaspoon
⅔ teaspoon
¾ teaspoon.............................. 4 ml
1 teaspoon .... 5 ml
1 ½ teaspoons .... 7 ml
1 ¾ teaspoons .... 9 ml
2 teaspoons............................ 10 ml

Tablespoon
1 tablespoon........................... 15 ml
1 ½ tablespoons...................... 22 ml
2 tablespoons .... 30 ml
3 tablespoons .... 45 ml
4 tablespoons .... 60 ml
5 tablespoons .... 75 ml
6 tablespoons .... 90 ml

Volume & Liquid
¼ cup .... 60 ml
⅓ cup...................................... 80 ml
½ cup .... 120 ml
⅔ cup .... 160 ml
¾ cup .... 180 ml
1 cup....................................... 240 ml
2 cups (1 pint) .... 480 ml
3 cups .... 710 ml
4 cups (32 oz) .... 960 ml
6 cups 48 oz. 1 ½ qt .... 1.5 L
8 cups 64 oz, ½ gal, 2 qts. .... 1.9 liter
16 cups, 1 gallon, (4 quarts) ..... 3.8 liter
2 gallons (8 quarts) .... 7.6 liter

Weight
½ ounce................................... 14 g
¾ ounce................................... 21 g
1 ounce .... 28 g
1.5 ounce .... 45 g
2 ounces.................................. 57 g
2.5 ounces............................... 70 g
3 ounces.................................. 84 g
3.5 ounces............................... 100 g
4 ounces.................................. 114 g
4.5 ounces............................... 128 g
5 ounces.................................. 143 g
5.5 ounces............................... 155 g
6 ounces.................................. 170 g
7 ounces.................................. 198 g
8 ounces.................................. 227 g
9 ounces .... 255 g
10 ounces................................. 280 g
11 ounces .... 312 g

12 ounces.................... 340 g
    Liquid 12 oz = 354 ml
13 ounces.................... 369 g
14 ounces.................... 396 g
15 ounces.................... 425 g
16 ounces.................... 454 g
    or 1 pound .... (.5 kg)
18 ounces.................... 510 g
20 ounces.................... 567 g
22 ounces.................... 624 g
24 ounces .... 680 g
26 ounces.................... 737 g
28 ounces.................... 794 g
32 ounces .... 1 kg
38 ounces.................... 1.1 kg
42 ounces.................... 1.2 kg
44 ounces.................... 1.25 kg
48 ounces.................... 1.3 kg
52 ounces.................... 1.4 kg
2 pounds .... 908 g
3 pounds .... 1.3 kg
4 pounds .... 1.8 kg
5 pounds .... 2.2 kg
6 pounds .... 2.7 kg
8 pounds .... 3.6 kg

Temperatures
°F.............................. °C
160° .... 71°
180° .... 82°
200° .... 93°
225° .... 107°
250° .... 121°
275° .... 135°
300° .... 148°
325° .... 162°
350° .... 176°
375° .... 190°
400° .... 204°
425° .... 220°
450° .... 230°
475° .... 250°

COOKBOOKS PUBLISHED BY COOKBOOK RESOURCES, LLC

The Ultimate Cooking
with 4 Ingredients

Easy Cooking with 5 Ingredients

The Best of Cooking
with 3 Ingredients

Gourmet Cooking with 5 Ingredients

Healthy Cooking with 4 Ingredients

Diabetic Cooking with 4 Ingredients

4-Ingredient Recipes for
30-Minute Meals

Essential 3-4-5 Ingredient Recipes

The Best 1001 Short, Easy Recipes

Easy Slow Cooker Cookbook

Easy One-Dish Meals

Easy Potluck Recipes

Essential Slow-Cooker Cooking

Quick Fixes with Cake Mixes

Casseroles to the Rescue

Easy Casseroles

Italian Family Cookbook

Sunday Night Suppers

365 Easy Meals

365 Easy Chicken

365 Soups and Stews

I Ain't On No Diet Cookbook

Kitchen Keepsakes/
More Kitchen Keepsakes

Old-Fashioned Cookies

Grandmother's Cookies

Mother's Recipes

Recipe Keeper

Cookie Dough Secrets

Gifts for the Cookie Jar

All New Gifts for the Cookie Jar

Gifts in a Pickle Jar

Muffins In A Jar

Brownies In A Jar

Cookie Jar Magic

Easy Desserts

Bake Sale Bestsellers

Quilters' Cooking Companion

Miss Sadie's Southern Cooking

Southern Family Favorites

Classic Tex-Mex and Texas Cooking

Classic Southwest Cooking

The Great Canadian Cookbook

The Best of Lone Star
Legacy Cookbook

Cookbook 25 Years

Pass the Plate

Texas Longhorn Cookbook

Trophy Hunters' Wild Game
Cookbook

Mealtimes and Memories

Holiday Recipes

Little Taste of Texas

Little Taste of Texas II

Southwest Sizzler

Southwest Olé

Class Treats

Leaving Home

To Order: **365 Easy Soups and Stews**

Please send _____ paperback copies @ $16.95 (U.S.) each $ _____

Texas residents add sales tax @ $1.36 each $ _____

Plus postage/handling @ $6.00 (1st copy) $ _____

$1.00 (each additional copy) $ _____

Check or Credit Card (Canada-credit card only) Total $ _____

Charge to: ❑ MasterCard   or   ❑ VISA

Account # _____

Expiration Date _____

Signature_____

Name _____

Address_____

City_____State_____Zip_____

Telephone (day_____(Evening)_____

| Mail or Call: |
| Cookbook Resources |
| 541 Doubletree Dr. |
| Highland Village, Texas 75077 |
| Toll Free (866) 229-2665 |
| (972) 317-6404 Fax |

To Order: **365 Easy Soups and Stews**

Please send _____ paperback copies @ $16.95 (U.S.) each $ _____

Texas residents add sales tax @ $1.36 each $ _____

Plus postage/handling @ $6.00 (1st copy) $ _____

$1.00 (each additional copy) $ _____

Check or Credit Card (Canada-credit card only) Total $ _____

Charge to: ❑ MasterCard   or   ❑ VISA

Account # _____

Expiration Date _____

Signature_____

Name _____

Address_____

City_____State_____Zip_____

Telephone (Day)_____(Evening)_____

| Mail or Call: |
| Cookbook Resources |
| 541 Doubletree Dr. |
| Highland Village, Texas 75077 |
| Toll Free (866) 229-2665 |
| (972) 317-6404 Fax |